An AutoCAD Workboo

An AutoCAD Workbook

A. Yarwood

Longman
Scientific &
Technical

Longman Scientific & Technical,
Longman Group UK Limited,
Longman House, Burnt Mill, Harlow,
Essex CM20 2JE, England,
and *Associated Companies throughout the world.*

First published 1991

British Library Cataloguing in Publication Data
Yarwood, A.
  An AutoCAD workbook.
  I. Title
  620

  ISBN 0–582–08803–8

Set in Linotron Melior 10/12pt

Produced by Longman Singapore Publishers (Pte) Ltd.
Printed in Singapore

Contents

viii   **Contents**

List of Plates (between pages 116 and 117)

Preface

The contents of this book are designed as a course of work for those wishing to learn how to use the CAD software AutoCAD. With the introduction of Release 11 of AutoCAD, an extension programme, the Advanced Modeling Extension (AME), was introduced. Details of 3-D solid model drawings produced with the aid of AME are included in Chapters 7 and 8. Also included (in Chapter 9) are descriptions of drawings produced for the stand-alone software AutoShade.

This book does not pretend to give complete and full descriptions of all the methods by which drawings can be constructed in AutoCAD. Practically any technical illustration which can be produced using hand methods can be drawn in AutoCAD. A much larger volume than this book would be required to include all of AutoCAD's many features. Only those which allow readers to achieve a reasonable standard of drawing with its aid are included here. Once readers have gained such a standard, their interest in this remarkable CAD software will become such as to compel further research into the commands, variables and methods available in AutoCAD.

All line drawings in this book have been constructed with the aid of AutoCAD 386, together with AME and AutoShade, working with an Epson AX3 (80386 CPU chip) computer, with 4 megabytes of extended memory. The drawings (both black line and colour plots) were plotted on a Roland plotter.

Drawing with CAD software has one great advantage over drawing by hand. This is the ability to produce drawings much more quickly. A good rule to follow in order to make maximum use of the speed with which drawings can be produced with CAD software is:

> Never draw the same thing twice.

This is because any drawing or part of a drawing can be arrayed, copied, dimensioned, inserted, moved, mirrored or rotated, without its having to be re-drawn. Another speed-of-drawing factor is the ability to add text in a variety of styles, easily and quickly, when working with CAD software such as AutoCAD.

Acknowledgements

The author wishes to acknowledge the permission given by Autodesk Ltd to reproduce drawings of the AutoCAD Release 11 tablet overlay (Chapter 5) and the menutree (Appendix B) from the Bonus/drawings disk of the AutoCAD 386 Release 11 software.

The author also wishes to acknowledge with grateful thanks the help given to him by members of staff of Autodesk Ltd.

The author and publishers acknowledge their appreciation to the British Standards Institute for permission to reproduce extracts from BS1192: Part 3: 1987. Complete copies can be obtained by post from BSI Sales, Linford Wood, Milton Keynes, MK14 6LE; telex 825777 BSIMK G.

Autodesk, AutoCAD, and AutoShade are registered as trademarks in the US Patent and Trademark Office by Autodesk, Inc.

IBM is a registered trademark of the International Business Machines Corporation.

MS–DOS is a registered trademark of the Microsoft Corporation.

A. Yarwood is a Registered Applications Developer with Autodesk Ltd.

CHAPTER 1

Introduction

The Work Examples in this book have been designed for constructing in an AutoCAD drawing editor configured for drawing on an A3 sheet size. If AutoCAD has not been configured in this way see Appendix A, which describes in detail how to prepare a drawing file which, when loaded, produces a suitable AutoCAD drawing editor screen on which the Work Examples can be drawn.

Starting up AutoCAD

When a PC (Personal Computer) in which AutoCAD is installed is switched on, it will automatically run its start-up procedures – self-testing circuits, disk drives, monitor, etc. and loading disk operating (DOS) files, system files, etc. When these procedures have been completed (10 to 15 seconds), the screen shows either a disk drive prompt such as C:\> or will display information in icon form or in textual form, depending upon which version of MS–DOS (Microsoft Disk Operating System) is in use. Before using AutoCAD for constructing drawings, the call-up procedure for loading AutoCAD files must be started. If a screen prompt such as C:\> appears, the usual method of loading AutoCAD is to type acad and press the Return key. After waiting for a few seconds, the AutoCAD Main Menu appears on screen (Fig. 1.1). Other screen displays appearing when a PC is switched on may require the selection of a word or an icon, with a pointing device such as a mouse or the typing in of a letter or word as prompted on the screen display.

Selection devices

Movements of the cursor cross-hairs in the AutoCAD drawing editor (Fig. 1.2) are under the control of a selection device. This may be one (or more) of the following:

```
                A U T O C A D
Copyright (C) 1982-1990  Autodesk, Inc. All Rights Reserved.
Release REL 11 (11/17/90) 386 DOS Extender
Serial Number: 99-111111


Main Menu

    0. Exit AutoCAD
    1. Begin a NEW drawing
    2. Edit an EXISTING drawing
    3. Plot a drawing
    4. Printer plot a drawing

    5. Configure AutoCAD
    6. File Utilities
    7. Compile shape/font description file
    8. Convert old drawing file
    9. Recover damaged drawing

Enter selection: 1

Enter NAME of drawing: a:\ex02_01
```

Fig. 1.1 The AutoCAD
Release 11 Main Menu

1. keyboard cursor keys – four keys with arrows – up, down, left, right;
2. a mouse;
3. a puck with a graphics tablet;
4. a stylus with a graphics tablet;
5. a joystick;
6. a trackerball.

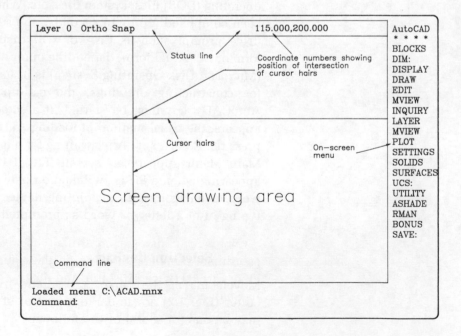

Fig. 1.2 The AutoCAD
drawing editor

Movements of the selection device are reflected on screen by movements of the cursor cross-hairs.

Pick and Return buttons

Whichever selection device is used, the position of the screen cursors can be picked by either pressing the keyboard Return (Enter) key when the keyboard is the selection device, or the pick button of other selection devices. Another button on some selection devices may respond in the same way as the keyboard Return (Enter) key.

Ctrl+C

AutoCAD constructs drawings with the aid of commands selected from menus, or typed at the keyboard. The selected, or typed, command appears at the command line in the AutoCAD drawing editor (Fig. 1.2). If a wrong command has been selected or if the operator wishes to cancel a command which is in operation, pressing the Ctrl key and key C together or holding down the Ctrl key and then pressing C cancels the current command.

Function keys

Several of the keyboard function keys (those with figures preceded by an F) allow short-cuts by switching some facilities on and off when pressed. These same facilities can also be switched by pressing the Ctrl key and certain letter keys. These key short-cuts are:

F1 – switches screen between drawing editor and an information screen
F6 – switches Coords on and off – also by Ctrl+D
F7 – switches Grid on and off – also by Ctrl+G
F8 – switches Ortho on and off – also by Ctrl+O
F9 – switches Snap on and off – also by Ctrl+B
F10 – switches Tablet on and off – also by Ctrl+T if a graphics tablet is attached.

Coords can also be controlled between absolute and relative coordinate numbers showing on the status line by pressing either F6 or Ctrl+D twice. Absolute and relative coordinates are discussed in Chapter 2.

The Snap function key control F9 is of particular value. If a point is to be picked which is precicely at a Snap point, switch Snap on. On other occasions it may be best to disable Snap by switching it off.

Work disk

If the computer at which you are working is in use by other people at other times, then it is best to prepare a work disk onto which and from which your work can be written and read. This disk will be a floppy disk and will normally be inserted in disk drive a:\ when you are working at the computer. Then all your work files will be loaded as NEW or as EXISTING drawings with the disk drive name a:\ before the file name.

Starting a Work Example

Before being able to construct the drawings for a Work Example, the following procedure will usually have to be followed:

1. switch the computer on;
2. start up AutoCAD;
3. when Main Menu appears on screen (Fig. 1.1), type 1 at the keyboard;
4. in answer to the prompt:

    Enter NAME of drawing:

    type a suitable drawing file name. In the example given in Fig. 1.1, the drawing file is to be on a disk in drive a:\, the filename is to be the abbreviation (ex) for Example, followed by the chapter number (02), then an underline (_) and finally the Work Example number (01). This form of filename is assumed throughout this book. Note that the drawing will be saved with a filename ex02_01.dwg – but the extension .dwg must not be included when giving a drawing filename in AutoCAD;
5. press Return. After a few seconds the AutoCAD drawing editor appears (Fig. 1.2).

    Note: If a suitable work file (see Appendix A) has been constructed, then from Main Menu select 2. When the prompt:

    Enter NAME of drawing:

    appears type the disk drive name and the filename work, in which case the prepared Work Example sheet drawing will appear in the AutoCAD drawing editor. An example would be:

    Enter NAME of drawing: a:\work *Keyboard Return*.

Terms used in the Work Examples

Throughout the sequences described in the Work Examples in this book, the following terms are used:

pick – position the cursor cross-hairs on the screen with the selection device and press the *pick* button of the device;

select – select an item such as a menu name or a command name from a menu by moving the cursor cross-hairs onto the name with the aid of the selection device;

Keyboard (or *Key*) – type the given figures, letters or words at the keyboard;

Return (or *Ret*) – press the *Return* or *Enter* key of the keyboard or the *Return* button of the selection device;

command – a command as it appears at the AutoCAD drawing editor command line;

on-screen menu – the menu which appears on the side of the AutoCAD drawing editor;

pull-down menu – a menu appearing from the selection of a menu name on the AutoCAD drawing editor's status line;

filenames – filenames for saving the drawings of Work Examples are given, e.g. *ex02_05*. Drawings with this given filename will be saved as *ex02_05.dwg*.

Menu names and command names throughout this book are printed in **bold** type – either in UPPER- or lower-case letters.

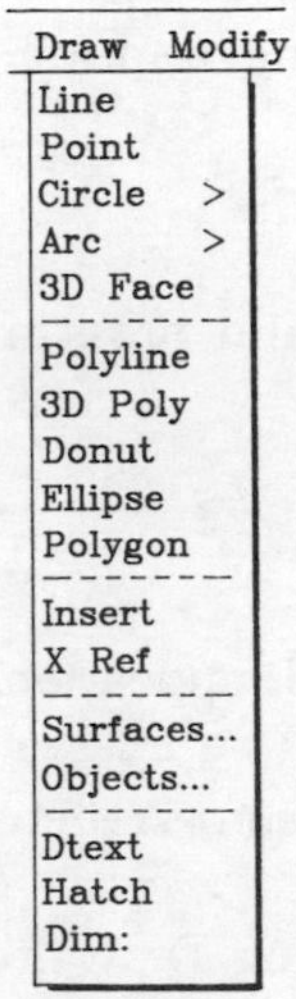

Trying out some commands in AutoCAD

Before attempting to construct the first of the Work Examples, experiment with the four command systems – Line, Circle, Arc and Dtext. Many technical drawings are composed completely of these four elements. Practising with these four commands will give a good basic introduction to drawing in AutoCAD. All four are in the pull-down menu Draw. This menu is shown in Fig. 1.3. Another set of commands that are very often used are the zoom commands. The zoom window and the zoom previous commands can also be practised at this stage. The zoom commands are in the pull-down menu Display (Fig. 1.4)

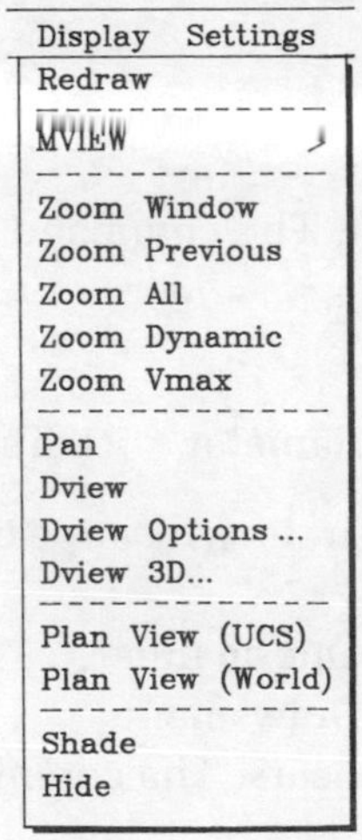

Follow the sequence:
1. switch the computer on;
2. start up AutoCAD;
3. when **Main Menu** appears on screen, type 1 at the keyboard;
4. in answer to the prompt:

Fig. 1.3 The Draw pull-down menu

Fig. 1.4 The Display pull-down menu

Enter NAME of drawing:

type a suitable drawing filename, e.g. a:\ex02_01;

5. press Return. After a few seconds the AutoCAD drawing editor appears;

6. move the selection device so that the cursor cross-hairs are in the status line. The status line changes to highlight nine pull-down menu names. Pick Draw from these names and press the pick button. The Draw menu appears on screen. Pick Line from this menu by moving the cross-hairs over the word Line and press the pick button. The following appears at the command line:

Command: line From point:

7. move the cursor to anywhere on screen and press the *pick* button. The Command line changes to:

Command : line From point:
To point:

8. pick another point on the screen. A line will appear on screen between the two picked points;

9. continue picking points anywhere on screen. A network of lines will appear;

10. start another series of lines by first picking Draw from the status line and then Line from the Draw menu.

11. pick Draw from the status line. Pick Circle from the Draw menu. Then pick Cen, Rad from the resulting Circle menu. The following appears at the command line:

Command:
CIRCLE 3P/2P/TTR/<Center point>:

12. pick any point on screen as a centre point. The command line changes to:

Command:
CIRCLE 3P/2P/TTR/<Center point>: Diameter/<Radius>:

13. pick any point for the circle radius. A circle will appear on screen;

14. press Return. Draw other circles in the same manner;

15. pick the Draw menu. Pick Arc from the Draw menu;

16. pick 3-point from the Arc menu which appears. The command line changes to:

> **Command:**
> **ARC Center/<Start point>:** *pick*
> **Center/End/<Second point>:** *pick*
> **End point:** *pick*

and an arc appears on screen at the picked points;

17. draw a series of arcs by selecting three points on each arc. Return must be pressed between each arc;
18. pick the Draw menu from the status line. Pick Dtext from the Draw menu. The command line changes to:

> **Command:**
> **Align/Fit/Center/Middle/Right/TL/TC/TR/ML/MC/MR/BL/ BC/BR:**

19. pick a start point for the text. The command line change to:

> **Rotation angle <0>:**

20. press Return, the command line changes to:

> **Text:**

type some words, which appear on screen as they are being typed.

21. press Return twice and the text is positioned on screen;
22. add further text to the screen with the Dtext command;
23. pick Display from the status line. The Display menu appears (Fig. 1.4). Pick Zoom Window from the Display menu. The command line changes to:

> **Command: zoom**
> **All/Center/Dynamic/Extents/Left/Previous/Window/**
> **<Scale(X)>:w**
> **First corner:**

pick any first corner position on screen. The command line changes to:

> **First corner: Other corner:**

24. pick the other corner and the screen zooms to the area within the chosen window;
25. pick Zoom Previous from the Draw menu. The screen reverts to its previous state;
26. practise zooming windows over various parts of the drawing.

Figure 1.5 shows the results of such an experiment at drawing lines, circles, arcs and text. Zooming part of the drawing in a zoom

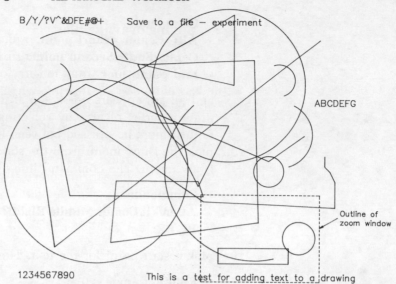

Fig. 1.5 Practise with commands from the Draw menu

window is shown in Fig. 1.6.

Note: The Work Examples throughout this book have been designed for those starting to learn how to use AutoCAD. In view of this, the more detailed systems in the AutoCAD software have not been included, e.g. descriptions and examples of the settings for variables both in AutoCAD itself and in the optional AME software, full details of dimensioning, the facilities for finding areas, volumes, material properties and the like.

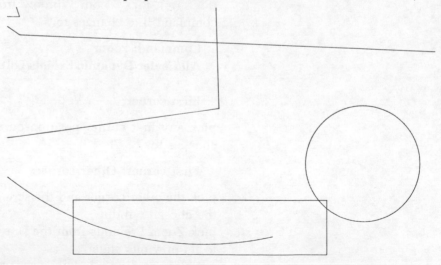

Fig. 1.6 The screen results of a Zoom window

Saving drawing files

As a drawing is being constructed it is advisable to SAVE it to disk every half-hour or so. Failure to carry out this operation may result in the loss of much of a drawing, when, e.g., electricity is cut off for any reason, a computer is switched off without saving the current drawing. If a fault such as this occurs, at least part of your work has been saved.

When the command SAVE is called, a dialogue box such as shown in Fig. 1.7 appears on screen. The filename of the drawing to be saved should be typed in the box next to the name File, followed by picking OK. The other boxes – Cancel, Type it (at the keyboard) or Default – may also be of use at times.

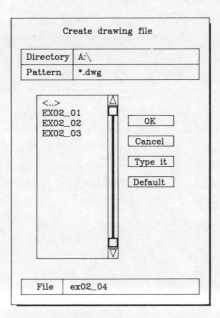

Fig. 1.7 The dialogue box Create drawing file

Methods of operation in AutoCAD

When an AutoCAD operator has become conversant with the variety of methods possible for constructing drawings with its aid, common practice is to use a variety of methods. Examples of this are:

1. key abbreviations for some commands (e.g. l for line) and select coordinate positions with a selection device;
2. select some commands from pull-down menus and others from on-screen menus and call some by keying commands or their abbreviations;

3. select commands from any available menu and also key most
    coordinates, but selecting some when it would be quicker to do
    so;
4. key abbreviations for some commands, select others from a
    graphics tablet, select positions on screen from the drawing
    editor area of the graphics tablet.

It is this possibility of using such a variety of methods when
operating with AutoCAD which helps to make it such a popular
CAD drawing instrument.

CHAPTER 2

Drawings from pull-down menus

Introduction

1. In the Work Examples it is assumed that the AutoCAD software in use has been configured so that the acad.dwg file will automatically load when choosing item:

    1. Begin a NEW drawing

    from AutoCAD's **Main Menu**;

2. and that a work disk for saving drawings has been inserted in drive a: of the computer.

Introduction to Work Example 2/1

Figures 2.1 and 2.2 show stages in the construction of Work Example 2/1. In Fig. 2.1, every intersection of lines and/or arcs in the drawing is given two numbers – a position number (1 to 18) and an x,y coordinate number – e.g. position 1 is (80,200). Do not include any of the letters or figures from Figs 2.1 or 2.2. Because COORDS is on, as the pointing device is moved, the x,y coordinates of cursor cross-hairs positions on screen will be shown as numbers on the status line at the top of the screen.

Notes on COORDS

1. When COORDS is on, the x,y coordinate numbers for the position of the intersection of the cursor cross-hairs shows on the status line.
2. If off, the numbers on the status line do not change when the cursor position is moved.
3. If showing relative coordinate numbers (page 14), a change to showing absolute coordinates (page 14) can be effected by pressing the Ctrl key and key D.

The sequence from item 2 below describes the selection of commands from pull-down menus.

Menu – The menu is selected by pointing at its name on the status line and then pressing the pick button of the selection device.

Command – The command name is selected by pointing at the name on the pull-down menu which appears and then pressing the pick button of the selection device.

Action – The action taken by the operator.

Return – Press the Return (Enter) key of the keyboard or the Return button of the selection device (puck, stylus or mouse).

Result – The result of the action taken.

To select each numbered position of Fig. 2.1, move the pointing device until the coordinate numbers on the status line agree with the coordinate positions of the required point in Fig. 2.1 and press the pick button of the selection device (puck, stylus or mouse).

Work Example 2/1

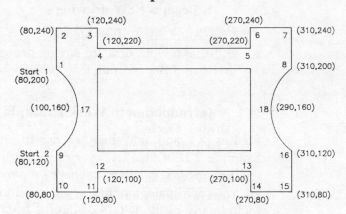

Fig. 2.1 First stage of Work Example 2/1

1. **Main Menu   1. Begin a NEW drawing**
   Enter selection: 1 *Keyboard Return*
   Enter NAME of drawing: a:\ex02_01 *Keyboard Return*
   When the AutoCAD drawing editor appears:
   (*Note:* numbers are as in Fig. 2.1).

Menu	*Command*	*Action*	*Result*
2. **Draw**	**Line**	*pick* 1	
		pick 2	
		pick 3	
		pick 4	
		pick 5	

Menu	Command	Action	Result
		pick 6	
		pick 7	
		pick 8	Upper straight lines drawn
3 **Draw**	**Line**	pick 9	
		pick 10	
		pick 11	
		pick 12	
		pick 13	
		pick 14	
		pick 15	
		pick 16	Lower straight lines drawn
4. **Draw**	**Arc**		
Arc	**3-point**	pick 1	
		pick 17	
		pick 9	Left-hand arc drawn
5. **Draw**	**Arc**		
Arc	**3-point**	pick 8	
		pick 18	
		pick 16	Right-hand arc drawn

Note: Numbers are as in Fig. 2.2

6. **Draw**	**Circle**		
Circle	**Cen, Rad**	pick 1	
		10 Keyboard Return	
7. **Draw**	**Circle**		
Circle	**Cen, Rad**	pick 2	
		10 Keyboard Return	

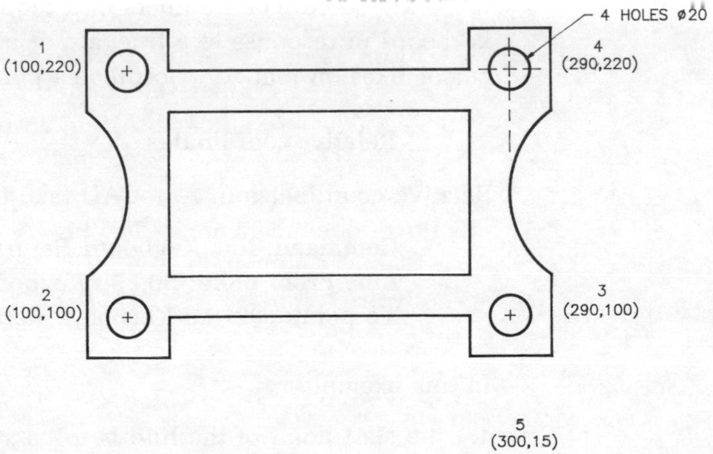

Fig. 2.2 Work Example 2/1

Menu	Command	Action	Result
8. **Draw**	**Circle**		
Circle	**Cen, Rad**	*pick 3*	
		10 *Keyboard Return*	
9. **Draw**	**Circle**		
Circle	**Cen, Rad**	*pick 4*	
		10 *Keyboard Return*	All 4 circles drawn
10. **Draw**	**Dtext**	*bl Keyboard Return*	
		pick 5	
		Work Example 2/2	
		Keyboard Return (twice)	Title added
11. **File**	**Save**	a:\ex02_01	Drawing saved to disk in drive a:\ as ex02_01.dwg

Introduction to Work Example 2/2

Figures 2.3 and 2.4 show two stages in the construction of Work Example 2/2. Do not include the numbers or letters given in Fig. 2.3.

When constructing Work Example 2/1, the positions of each intersection of lines or lines and arcs were picked by pointing at the x,y coordinate positions of the cursor as given by the coordinate numbers on the status line as the selection device was moved. In this Work Example the lengths of lines will be entered at the command line as absolute or as relative coordinates.

Absolute coordinates

If the x,y coordinate numbers of a required point are typed at the keyboard in response to a line, arc or circle command prompt, the cursor fixes on that x,y coordinates point.

Relative coordinates

Relative coordinates in AutoCAD take the form:

> **Command: line** *Keyboard Return*
> **Line From point:** 50,250 *Keyboard Return*
> **To point:** @270,0 *Keyboard Return*

In this example

1. the start point of the line is to be x,y = 50,250;

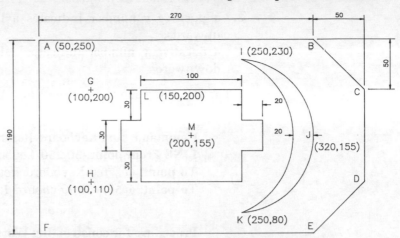

Fig. 2.3 First stage of Work Example 2/2

2. the symbol @ states that what follows are to be relative coordinate numbers;
3. 270 is the unit length of the line along the x axis (horizontally on screen);
4. 0 is the unit length in the direction of the y axis (vertically on screen).

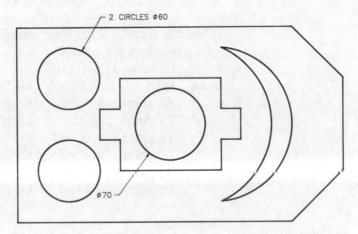

Fig. 2.4 Work Example 2/2

The example above shows how the line AB of Fig. 2.3 would be drawn using the relative coordinates method.

Notes

1. a positive x number indicates the line is to be drawn horizontally to the right;
2. a negative x number indicates a line to be drawn horizontally to the left;

3. a positive y number indicates a line to be drawn vertically upwards;

4. a negative y number indicates a line to be drawn vertically downwards.

The following shows how the lines AB and BC of Fig. 2.3 can be drawn using the relative coordinates method:

Command: line *Keyboard Return*
LINE From point: 50,250 *Keyboard Return*
To point: @270,0 *Keyboard Return*
To point: @50,−50 *Keyboard Return*

Procedure for constructing Work Example 2/2

All commands are selected from the named pull-down menus.

Work Example 2/2

1. **Main Menu** **1. Begin a NEW drawing**
   Enter selection: 1 *Keyboard Return*
   Enter NAME of drawing: a:\ex02_02 *Keyboard Return*

When the AutoCAD drawing editor appears:
(*Note*: numbers are as in Fig. 2.3)

Menu	Command	Action		Result
2. **Draw**	**Line**	50,250	*Keyboard Return*	
	To point:	@270,0	*Keyboard Return*	
	To point:	@50,−50	*Keyboard Return*	
	To point:	@0,−90	*Keyboard Return*	
	To point:	@−50,−50	*Keyboard Return*	
	To point:	@−270,0	*Keyboard Return*	
	To point:	c (close)	*Keyboard Return*	ABCDEF drawn
3. **Draw**	**Line**	150,200	*Keyboard Return*	
	To point:	@100,0	*Keyboard Return*	
	To point:	@0,−30	*Keyboard Return*	
	To point:	@20,0	*Keyboard Return*	
	To point:	@0,−30	*Keyboard Return*	
	To point:	@−20,0	*Keyboard Return*	
	To point:	@0,−30	*Keyboard Return*	
	To point:	@−100,0	*Keyboard Return*	
	To point:	@0,30	*Keyboard Return*	
	To point:	@−20,0	*Keyboard Return*	

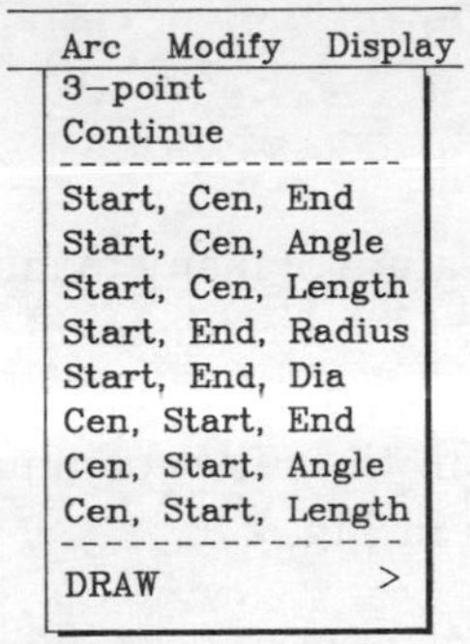

```
Arc   Modify   Display
┌─────────────────────────┐
│ 3-point                 │
│ Continue                │
├─────────────────────────┤
│ Start, Cen, End         │
│ Start, Cen, Angle       │
│ Start, Cen, Length      │
│ Start, End, Radius      │
│ Start, End, Dia         │
│ Cen, Start, End         │
│ Cen, Start, Angle       │
│ Cen, Start, Length      │
├─────────────────────────┤
│ DRAW              >     │
└─────────────────────────┘
```

Fig. 2.5 The Arc pull-down
sub menu

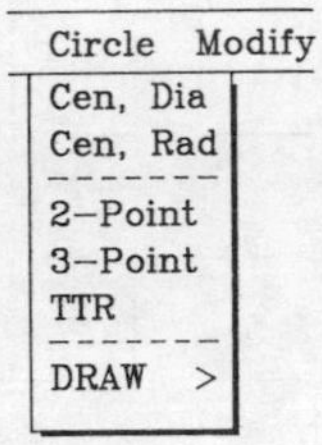

```
Circle   Modify
┌─────────────────┐
│ Cen, Dia        │
│ Cen, Rad        │
├─────────────────┤
│ 2-Point         │
│ 3-Point         │
│ TTR             │
├─────────────────┤
│ DRAW     >      │
└─────────────────┘
```

Fig. 2.6 The Circle
pull-down sub menu

	Menu	Command	Action	Result
	To point:	@0,30	*Keyboard Return*	
	To point:	@20,0	*Keyboard Return*	
	To point:	c (close)	*Keyboard Return*	Central shape drawn
4.	**Draw** **Arc**			
	Arc **3-point**	250,230	*Keyboard Return*	
		320,155	*Keyboard Return*	
		250,80	*Keyboard Return*	One arc drawn
5.	**Draw** **Arc**			
	Arc **3-point**	250,230	*Keyboard Return*	
		300,155	*Keyboard Return*	
		250,80	*Keyboard Return*	Second arc drawn
6.	**Draw** **Circle**			
	Circle **Cen, Rad**	100,200	*Keyboard Return*	
		30	*Keyboard Return*	One circle drawn
7.	**Draw** **Circle**			
	Circle **Cen, Dia**	100,110	*Keyboard Return*	
		60	*Keyboard Return*	Second circle drawn
8.	**Draw** **Circle**			
	Circle **Cen, Dia**	200,155	*Keyboard Return*	
		70	*Keyboard Return*	Third circle drawn
9.	**Draw** **Dtext**	bl	*Keyboard Return*	
		305,15	*Keyboard Return*	
		Work	*Keyboard Return*	Title
		Example	(twice)	added
		2/2		
10.	**File** **Save**	a:	*Keyboard Return*	Drawing saved to disk in drive a:\ as ex02_02. dwg
		\ex02_02		

Introduction to Work Example 2/3

Fillet

Fillets – radiused corners – are a common feature of many technical drawings. The AutoCAD command Fillet allows fillets of any radius to be automatically drawn at the joins of straight lines and/or arcs. This Work Drawing gives practice with the Fillet command. The completed Work Example is as shown in Fig. 2.8.

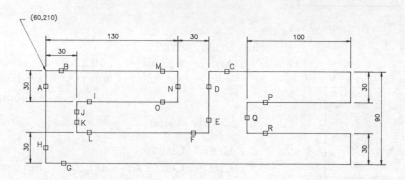

Fig. 2.7 First Stage of Example 2/3

Work Example 2/3

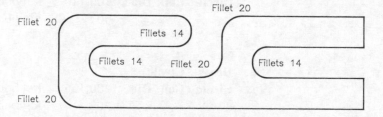

Fig. 2.8 Work Example 2/3

1.   **Main Menu   1. Begin a NEW drawing**
         Enter selection: 1 *Keyboard Return*
         Enter NAME of drawing: a:\ex02_03 *Keyboard Return*
     When the AutoCAD drawing editor appears:

Start by constructing the drawing Fig. 2.7 in the AutoCAD drawing editor with the aid of the command Line from the pull-down Draw menu. To construct an accurate drawing, use both the absolute coordinate and the relative coordinate methods of drawing lines at correct unit lengths and positions as was used when constructing Work Exercise 2. When this outline drawing has been constructed, then complete the drawing as shown in Fig. 2.8.

Menu	Command	Action		Result
2. **Modify**	**Fillet**	r (Radius)	Keyboard Return	
		20	Keyboard Return	
		Return (Yes – second time)		
		pick A		
		pick B	Return	Fillet formed
		pick C		
		pick D	Return	Fillet formed
		pick E		
		pick F	Return	Fillet formed
		pick G		
		pick H	Return	Fillet formed
3. **Modify**	**Fillet**	r (Radius)	Keyboard Return	
		14	Keyboard Return	
		Return (Yes – second time)		
		pick I		
		pick J	Return	Fillet formed
		pick K		
		pick L	Return	Fillet formed
		pick M		
		pick N	Return	Fillet formed
		pick N		
		pick O	Return	Fillet formed
		pick P		
		pick Q	Return	Fillet formed
		pick Q		
		pick R	Return	Fillet formed
4. **Draw**	**Dtext**	bl	Keyboard Return	
		305, 15	Keyboard Return	
		Work	Keyboard Return	Title
		Example	(twice)	added
		2/3		

Menu	Command	Action		Result
5. **File**	**Save**	a:\ex02_03	*Keyboard Return*	Drawing saved to disk in drive a:\ as *ex02_03. dwg*

Introduction to Work Example 2/4

Circles tangential to each other and trimming

A feature common to many technical drawings is that of circles in contact with each other at their respective tangential points. In AutoCAD the TTR option of the Circle command is available for ensuring that such adjoining circles are accurately joined at their tangential points.

This exercise allows practice in the use of the Circle TTR command. It also gives practice in using the Trim command for

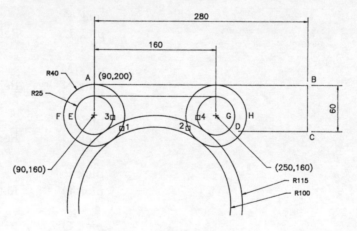

Fig. 2.9 First stage of Work Example 2/4

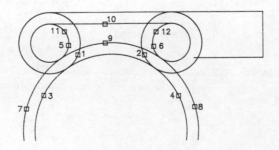

Fig. 2.10 Second stage of Work Example 2/4

ensuring that lines, circles and arcs meet each other at precise intersections. The completed Work Exercise is as shown in Fig. 2.12.

Start by constructing the drawing Fig. 2.9 with the aid of the commands Line and Circle from the pull-down Draw menu. Use the absolute coordinate and the relative coordinate methods of drawing lines and circles which are accurately positioned as was used when constructing Work Exercises 2 and 3. Then trim circles and lines as shown in Fig. 2.10 with the Trim command from the Modify menu to produce the outline given by Fig. 2.11. Finally add fillets and the circle as shown in Fig. 12.

Work Example 2/4

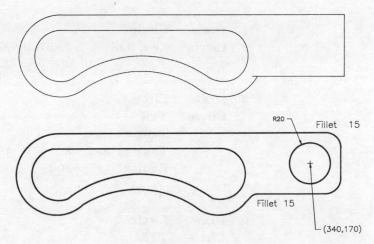

Fig. 2.11 Third stage of Work Example 2/4

Fig. 2.12 Work Example 2/4

1. **Main Menu   1. Begin a NEW drawing**
    Enter selection: 1 *Keyboard Return*
    Enter NAME of drawing: a:\ex02_04 *Keyboard Return*

When the AutoCAD drawing editor appears:

	Menu	Command	Action		Result
2.	**Draw**	**Line**	90,200	*Keyboard Return*	
		To point:	@280,0	*Keyboard Return*	
		To point:	@0,−60	*Keyboard Return*	
		To point:	@−100,0	*Keyboard Return*	
				Return	AB, BC, CD drawn
3.	**Draw**	**Line**	90,185	*Keyboard Return*	

Menu	Command	Action		Result
		250,185	*Keyboard Return*	Line XX drawn
4. **Draw**	**Circle**			
Circle	**Cen, Rad**	90,160	*Keyboard Return*	
		25	*Keyboard Return*	Circle E drawn
5. **Draw**	**Circle**			
Circle	**Cen, Rad**	250,160	*Keyboard Return*	
		25	*Keyboard Return*	Circle G drawn
6. **Draw**	**Circle**			
Circle	**Cen, Rad**	90,160	*Keyboard Return*	
		40	*Keyboard Return*	Circle F drawn
7. **Draw**	**Circle**			
Circle	**Cen, Rad**	250,160	*Keyboard Return*	
		40	*Keyboard Return*	Circle H drawn
8. **Draw**	**Circle**			
Circle	**TTR**			
	Tangent spec	1	*pick*	
	Tangent spec	2	*pick*	
	Radius	100	*Keyboard Return*	Circle R 100 drawn
9. **Draw**	**Circle**			
Circle	**TTR**			
	Tangent spec	3	*pick*	
	Tangent spec	4	*pick*	
	Radius	115	*Keyboard Return*	Circle R 115 drawn

Letters and figures as in Fig. 2.10

10. **Modify**	**Trim**				
	Select objects	1	*pick*		
	Select objects	2	*pick*	*Return*	
	Object to trim	3	*pick*	*Return*	Circle 3,4 trimmed
11. **Modify**	**Trim**				
	Select objects	5	*pick*		
	Select objects	6	*pick*	*Return*	

Menu	Command	Action		Result
	Object to trim	7 *pick*		
	Object to trim	8 *pick*	*Return*	Circle 7,8 trimmed
12. **Modify**	**Trim**			
	Select objects	0 *pick*		
	Select objects	10 *pick*	*Return*	
	Object to trim	11 *pick*		
	Object to trim	12 *pick*	*Return*	Circles 11 and 12 trimmed

Figures as in Fig. 2.12

13. **Modify**	**Fillet**	r (Radius)	*Keyboard*	
		15	*Return* (yes twice)	
	Select objects	Select lines and arcs as necessary		Fillets formed
14. **Draw**	**Circle**			
	Circle	**Cen, Rad**		
		340,170	*Keyboard Return*	
		20	*Keyboard Return*	Circle drawn
15. **Draw**	**Dtext**	bl	*Keyboard Return*	
		300,15	*Keyboard Return*	
		Work	*Keyboard Return*	
		Example	(twice)	Title
		2/4		added
16. **File**	**Save**	a:\	*Keyboard Return*	
		ex02_04		Drawing saved in drive a:\ as *ex02_04. dwg*

Introduction to Work Example 2/5

The command Mirror

The time taken to construct a drawing which is symmetrical about an axis can be greatly reduced by making use of the command Mirror. Mirror is found in the pull-down menu Modify (Fig. 2.13).

Figure 2.15 is an example of a drawing constructed with the aid of the Mirror command. The first stages of constructing the drawing

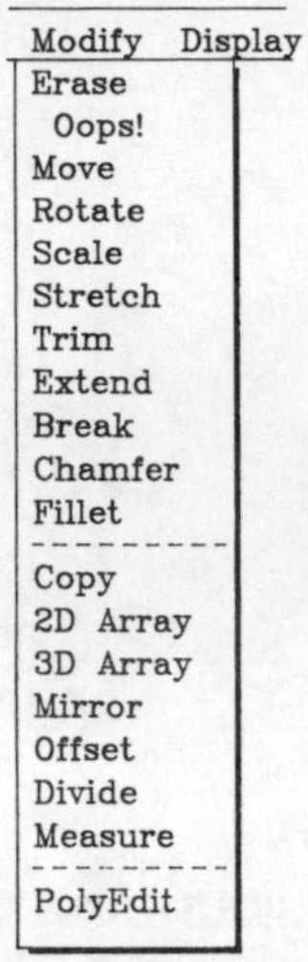

```
Modify   Display
  Erase
   Oops!
  Move
  Rotate
  Scale
  Stretch
  Trim
  Extend
  Break
  Chamfer
  Fillet
  ----------
  Copy
  2D Array
  3D Array
  Mirror
  Offset
  Divide
  Measure
  ----------
  PolyEdit
```

Fig. 2.13 The Modify pull-down menu

are given in Fig. 2.14. Letters, figures and dimensions as in Fig. 2.14, Stage 1.

Work Example 2/5

1. **Main Menu 1. Begin a NEW drawing**
   Enter selection: 1 *Keyboard Return*
   Enter NAME of drawing: a:\ex02_05 *Keyboard Return*

When the AutoCAD drawing editor appears:

Menu	Command	Action		Result
2. **Draw**	**Line**	70,160	*Keyboard Return*	
	To point:	@0,20	*Keyboard Return*	
	To point:	@45,0	*Keyboard Return*	
		Return		Left part drawn
3. **Draw**	**Line**	115,160	*Keyboard Return*	
	To point:	@0,55	*Keyboard Return*	
	To point:	@175,0	*Keyboard Return*	
	To point:	@0,−55	*Keyboard Return*	
		Return		Centre part drawn
4. **Draw**	**Line**	290,180	*Keyboard Return*	
	To point:	@35,0	*Keyboard Return*	
	To point:	@0,−20	*Keyboard Return*	
		Return		Right part drawn
5. **Draw**	**Arc**			
Arc	**3-point**	190,215	*pick*	
		145,205	*pick*	
		115,185	*pick*	Arc drawn
6. **Modify**	**Trim**			
	Select objects:	*pick* arc	Return	
	Objects to trim:	*pick* lines	Return	Lines trimmed

Letters and dimensions as in Fig. 2.14, Stage 2

7. **Modify Chamfer**   d
   (Distance) Return

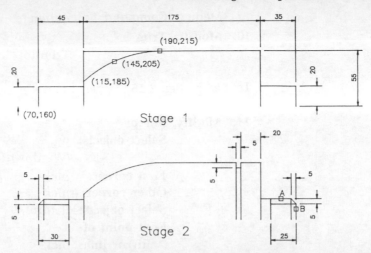

Fig. 2.14 First stages of Work Example 2/5

Menu	Command	Action		Result
	First distance: 5	*Keyboard Return*		
	Second distance: 5	*Keyboard Return*		
	First line: *pick* A			
	Second line: *pick* B			Right chamfer drawn
8. **Modify**	**Chamfer**			
		Repeat for left chamfer		
9. **Draw**	**Line**			
		Add new lines as in Stage 2 drawing		

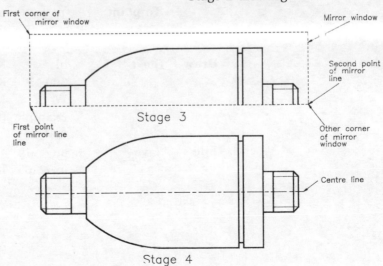

Fig. 2.15 Work Example 2/5

Menu	Command	Action	Result
10. **Modify**	**Trim**		
		Trim top line of groove	

Text as in Fig. 2.15, Stages 3 and 4

11. **Modify**	**Mirror**		
	Select objects:	w	
		(Window)*Return*	
	First corner:	*pick*	
	Other corner:	*pick*	
	Select objects:	*Return*	
	First point of mirror line	*pick*	
	Second point:	*pick*	
	Delete old objects? <N>:	*Return*	Second half of drawing appears
12. **Settings**	**Layer Control**	Centre **current**	
		pick **OK**	Layer Centre now current layer
13. **Draw**	**Line**	*pick*	end of line
	To point	*pick*	other end
			Centre line drawn
14. **Draw**	**Dtext**	bl	*Keyboard Return*
		300,15	*Keyboard Return*
		Work	*Keyboard Return*	Title
		Example	(twice)	added
		2/5		
15. **File**	**Save**	a:\	
		ex02_05	*Keyboard Return*	Drawing saved in drive a:\ as ex02_05. dwg

Introduction to Work Example 2/6

The commands Text and Dtext

Most drawings contain some text. AutoCAD files contain a variety of text fonts which can be set to any size, slope or angle. In this Work Example three fonts – scriptc, romanc and italicc – are employed. The difference between Dtext and Text is that Dtext appears on screen as it is being typed at the command line. Text does not appear on screen until it has been typed at the command line and Return pressed.

Work Example 2/6

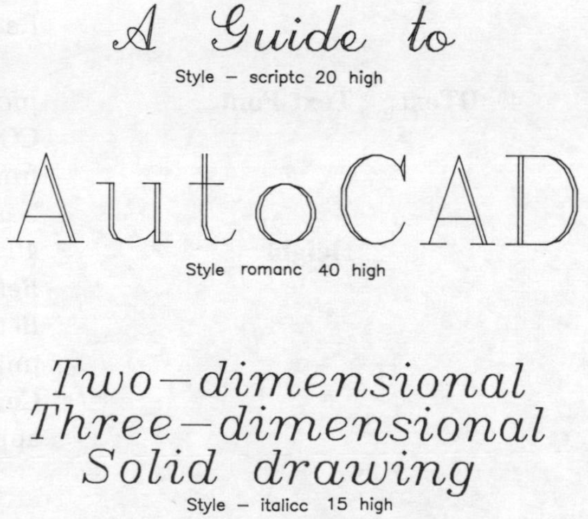

A Guide to

Style – scriptc 20 high

AutoCAD

Style romanc 40 high

Two–dimensional
Three–dimensional
Solid drawing

Style – italicc 15 high

Fig. 2.16 First stage of Work Example 2/6

Text as in Fig. 2.16

1. **Main Menu   1. Begin a NEW drawing**
   Enter selection: 1 *Keyboard Return*
   Enter NAME of drawing: a:\ex02_06 *Keyboard Return*

When the AutoCAD drawing editor appears:

Menu	Command	Action	Result
2. **Options**			
DTEXT			
OPTIONS			
DText	**Text Font**	pick **SCRIPT COMPLEX** from dialogue box	

		Height	20 *Keyboard* *Return* *Return – press* until **Command:** appears	Style set to scriptc, 20 units high
3.	**Draw** **Dtext**	bl **Bottom/left point** **Height <20>:** **Rotation angle <0>:** **Text**	*Keyboard Return* *pick* *Return* *Return* A Guide to *Keyboard* *Return* (twice)	Text appears on screen
4.	**DText**	**Text Font** **Height**	*pick* **ROMAN COMPLEX** from dialogue box 40 *Keyboard* *Return* *Return – press* until **Command:** appears	Style set to romanc, 40 units high
5.	**Draw** **Dtext**	bl **Bottom/left point** **Height <40>:** **Rotation angle <0>:** **Text**	*Keyboard* *Return* *pick* *Return* *Return* AutoCAD *Keyboard* *Return* (twice)	Text appears on screen
6.	**DText**	**Text Font** **Height:**	*pick* **ITALIC COMPLEX** from dialogue box 15 *Keyboard* *Return* *Return – press*	

				until
				Command:
				appears	Style set to italicc, 15 units high

7	**Draw**	bl	*Keyboard*	
	Dtext		*Return*	
		Bottom/left point	*pick*	
		Height <15>:	*Return*	
		Rotation angle <0>:	*Return*	
		Text	Two-dimensional *Keyboard*	
			Return (twice)	Text appears on screen
			Three-dimensional *Keyboard*	
			Return	Text appears on screen
			Solid drawing *Keyboard*	
			Return (twice)	Text appears on screen

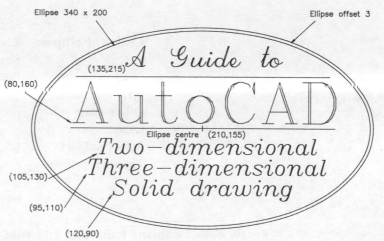

Fig. 2.17 Work Example 2/6

Text and numbers as in Fig. 2.17

Menu	Command	Action	Result
8. **Modify**	**Move**		
	Select objects:	pick scriptc text Return	
	Base point:	pick start of text Return	
	Second point:	pick 135,215 Return	Text moved
9. **Modify**	**Move**		
	Select objects:	pick romanc text Return	
	Base point:	pick start of text Return	
	Second point:	pick 80,160 Return	Text moved
10. **Modify**	**Move**		
	Select objects:	pick italicc text Return	
	Base point:	pick start of text Return	
	Second point:	pick 105,130 Return	Text moved

11 to 13 Move the other two italicc texts in the same way

Menu	Command	Action	Result
14. **Ellipse**	Keyboard Return		
	Center:	c (Centre) Keyboard Return	
	Center of ellipse:	210,155 Keyboard Return	
	Axis endpoint:	pick 40,155	
	Other axis:	pick 210,255	Ellipse appears
15. **Modify**	**Offset**		
	Select subject:	pick ellipse	
	Through point:	pick point about 3 units from ellipse	Second ellipse appears

16. Select Romans fount and add title with **Dtext** (Draw) – Work Example 2/6

	Menu	Command	Action	Result
			Return (twice)	Title added
17.	**File**	**Save**	a:\ex02_06	
			Keyboard	
			Return	Drawing saved in drive a:\ as ex02_06.dwg

CHAPTER 3

Drawing by commands typed at keyboard

Introduction

The Work Examples in this chapter deal with the construction of drawings with as many commands and responses typed directly at the keyboard as is possible. Some picking of points and objects on the screen will also be included.

Command abbreviations

When working with standard AutoCAD Release 11 software, a file acad.pgp will have been automatically loaded when the software is loaded. This file allows a number of abbreviations for commands to be typed at the keyboard, rather than having to type the whole command. The abbreviations can be typed, either in lower-case or in capital letters. These command abbreviations will be used in the Work Sequences in this chapter. They are:

A – ARC
C – CIRCLE
CP – COPY
E – ERASE
L – LINE
LA – LAYER
M – MOVE
P – PAN
PL – PLINE
R – REDRAW
Z – ZOOM
B – BREAK
F – FILLET
T – TEXT
S – STYLE

There are some other abbreviations in acad.pgp for 3D constructions. As this chapter is only concerned with 2D constructions, these have not been included in the above list.

Response abbreviations

In addition to the above command abbreviations, many of the responses to prompts can be typed in an abbreviated form. As with the command abbreviations, these can also be keyed in lower-case or in capital letters. Some examples of the response abbreviations are:

> a – all
> c – centre
> w – window
> p – previous

Other response abbreviations will be peculiar to particular commands. Where these occur in the Work Example sequences, they will be shown and used. The abbreviations for responses are always shown with the prompts – the capital letters are the abbreviations. As an example, when the command LAYER is called, the first prompt is:

?/Make/Set/New/ON/OFF/Color/Ltype/Freeze/Thaw:

The abbreviations in response to this prompt could be any of the following:

> m for Make; s for Set; N for New; c for Color;
> L for Ltype; f for Freeze; T for Thaw.

The Return key

When commands or responses are typed at the keyboard, they will not become effective until the keyboard's *Return* (Enter) key has been pressed. In this chapter, it is assumed that this is understood by the reader and the statement *Keyboard Return* will not be included in the sequence instructions. Despite this, it may be necessary at times to show the Return response, when it is the only response possible to achieve the required construction result.

Work Example sequences

In this chapter the sequences take the form:

Command/prompt   *Response Result*
Command: l (line)
From point: 100,100
To point: 100,200
To point: 200,200
To point: 200,100
To point: c (close)
Command: Square drawn

In this example:

1. the letter l is typed, followed by pressing the *Return* key. The full meaning of the abbreviation – line – is given in brackets;
2. the figures, e.g. 100,100, are typed, followed by pressing the *Return* key;
3. the c is typed, followed by pressing the *Return* key.

Where it is obvious what is required as a response, only part of a prompt is shown. As an example, take the command

CIRCLE:
Command: c (circle)
3P/2P/TTR/<Center point>:

As it will usually only be necessary to determine the centre point, the prompt **3P/2P/TTR/<Center point>:** will be shown only as **<Center point>:** in the sequences below.

Introduction to Work Example 3/1

This Work Example describes the construction of a simple three-view Third Angle orthographic projection. The construction is drawn on four layers – outlines on layer 0; hidden detail on layer HIDDEN; centre lines on layer CENTRE; text on layer TEXT. The constructions include making of three of these layers. Do not include any of the dimensions given in the drawings associated with this Example. The outlines are all drawn with plines (polylines) of a thickness 0.7. This allows the outlines to be printed or plotted as thicker lines than hidden detail or centre lines.

Work Example 3/1

Stage 1 (Fig. 3.1)

1. **Main Menu   1. Begin a NEW drawing**
                Enter selection: 1

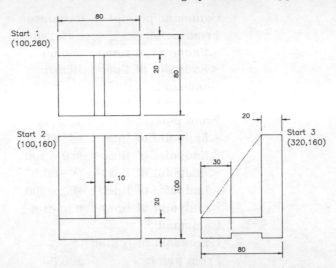

Fig. 3.1 First stage of Work
Example 3/1

Enter NAME of drawing: a:\ex03_01

When the AutoCAD drawing editor appears:

Command/prompt	Response	Result
2. **Command:** pl (pline)		
From point:	100,260	
Arc/Close/Halfwidth/		
Length/Undo/Width/		
<Endpoint of line>:	w (width)	
Starting width <0>:	0.7	
Ending width <0>:	0.7	Pline width now set at 0.7
<Endpoint of line>:	@80,0	
<Endpoint of line>:	@0,−80	
<Endpoint of line>:	@−80,0	
<Endpoint of line>:	c (close)	
Command:		Square of plan drawn
3. **Command:** pl (pline)		
From point:	100,240	
<Endpoint of line>:	@80,0	
<Endpoint of line>:	Return	
Command:		Back of plan
4. **Command:** pl (pline)		
From point:	135,180	
<Endpoint of line>	@0,60	
<Endpoint of line>	Return	
Command:		Web of plan
5. **Command:** pl (pline)		

Command/prompt	Response	Result
From point:	145,180	
<Endpoint of line>:	@0,60	
<Endpoint of line>:	Return	
Command:		Plan completed

6. **Command:** pl (pline)

From point:	100,160	
<Endpoint of line>:	@80,0	
<Endpoint of line>:	@0,−100	
<Endpoint of line>:	@−80,0	
<Endpoint of line>:	@0.−100	
<Endpoint of line>:	c (close)	
Command:		Rectangle of front view

7. **Command:** pl (pline)

From point:	100,80	
<Endpoint of line>:	@80,0	
<Endpoint of line>:	Return	
Command:		Base of front view

8. **Command:** pl (pline)

From point:	135,160	
<Endpoint of line>:	@0,−80	
<Endpoint of line>:	Return	
Command:		Web of front view

9. **Command:** pl (pline)

From point:	145,160	
<Endpoint of line>:	@0,−80	
<Endpoint of line>:	Return	
Command:		Front view drawn

10. **Command:** pl (pline)

From point:	320,160	
<Endpoint of line>:	@−20,0	
<Endpoint of line>:	@0,−80	
<Endpoint of line>:	@−60,0	
<Endpoint of line>:	@0,−20	
<Endpoint of line>:	@30,0	
<Endpoint of line>:	@0,5	
<Endpoint of line>:	@30,0	
<Endpoint of line>:	@0,−5	
<Endpoint of line>:	@20,0	
<Endpoint of line>:	c (close)	
Command:		Outline end view

11. **Command:** pl (pline)

From point:	300,160	
<Endpoint of line>:	@−60,−80	

Command/prompt	Response	Result
<Endpoint of line>:	*Return*	
Command:		End view drawn
12. **Command:** save	a:\ex03_01	Drawing saved

Stage 2 (Fig. 3.2)

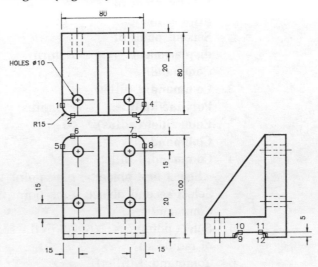

Fig. 3.2 Work Example 3/1

1. **Command:** pl (pline)
   From point: 110,195
   <Endpoint of line>: a (arc)
   <Endpoint of arc>: s (second)
   Second point: 115,200
   Endpoint: 120,195
   <Endpoint of arc>: s (second)
   Second point: 115,190
   Endpoint: 110,195
   <Endpoint of arc>: Return
   Command: One hole drawn
2. **Command:** cp (copy)
   Select objects *pick pline circle*
   1 selected, 1 found
   Select objects: *Return*
   <Base point of displacement>/
   Multiple: m (multiple)
   Base point: 115,195
   Second point of displacement: 160,195
   Second point of

displacement:	115,145	
Second point of		
displacement:	115,95	
Second point of		
displacement:	165,145	
Second point of		
displacement:	165,95	
Second point of		
displacement:	*Return*	
Command:		All holes drawn

3. **Command:** f (fillet)
    Polyline/Radius: r (radius)
    Enter fillet radius): 10
    Command:

4. **Command:** f (fillet)
    <Select first object>: *pick* point 1
    Select second object: *pick* point 2
    Command: One fillet drawn

5. Select points 3,4; 5,6; 7,8 in the same way to draw other fillets of radius 10

6. **Command:** f (fillet)
    Polyline/Radius: r (radius)
    Enter fillet radius): 4
    Command:

7. **Command:** f (fillet)
    <Select first object>: *pick* point 9
    Select second object: *pick* point 10
    Command: One fillet drawn

8. Draw fillet 11,12 of radius 4 in the same way. A ZOOM window may be needed for this

9. **Command:** save   a:\ex03_01   Drawing saved

Stage 3 (Fig. 3.2)

1. **Command:** ltscale (Linetype scale)
    New scale factor <1>:0.5
    Command: Set linetype scale
                              suitable for A3

2. **Command:** la (layer)
    Make/Set/New/ON/
    OFF/Color/Ltype/
    Freeze/Thaw: m (make)
    New current layer
    <0>:   hidden
    Make/Set/New/ON/

OFF/Color/Ltype/		
Freeze/Thaw:	c (color)	
Color:	red	
Layer name for color		
1 (red) <HIDDEN>:	*Return*	
Make/Set/New/ON/		
OFF/Color/Ltype/		
Freeze/Thaw:	l (linetype)	
Linetype:	hidden	
Layer name for		
linetype HIDDEN		
<HIDDEN>:	*Return*	
Make/Set/New/ON/		
OFF/Color/Ltype/		
Freeze/Thaw:	*Return*	Layer HIDDEN made and also current

3. **Command:** l (line)

From point:	110,260	
To point:	@0,−20	
To point:*Return*		
Command:		One hidden line drawn

4. **Command:** cp (copy)

Select objects	*pick hidden line*	
1 selected, 1 found		
Select objects:	*Return*	
<Base point of		
displacement>/		
Multiple:	m (multiple)	
Base point:	110,260	
Second point of		
displacement:	120,260	
Second point of		
displacement:	160,260	
Second point of		
displacement:	170,260	
Second point of		
displacement:	120,80	
Second point of		
displacement:	130,80	
Second point of		
displacement:	160,80	
Second point of		
displacement:	170,80	

Command/prompt	Response	Result
Second point of displacement:	250,80	
Second point of displacement:	260,80	
Second point of displacement:	Return	
Command:		vertical hidden lines drawn

5. Draw the four horizontal hidden lines in the same manner –
   first draw one line and then copy the other three
6. Make a layer CENTRE, of colour green and linetype centre in a
   similar manner to the making of the layer HIDDEN. When
   made, the layer Centre becomes the current layer
7. **Command:** l (line)

From point:	115,265	
To point:	@0,−30	
To point:	Return	
Command:		

8. Copy the vertical centre line to other positions for vertical
   centre lines in a similar manner to the copying of the vertical
   hidden detail lines
9. Draw a horizontal centre line from 295,145 to @30,0 and copy
   to other horizontal centre line positions
10. **Command:** save   a:\ex03_01   Drawing saved

Stage 4 (Fig. 3.2)

1. Set layer 0 as the current layer
   Command: la (layer)

Make/Set/New/ON/ OFF/Color/Ltype/ Freeze/Thaw:	s (set)	
New current layer:	0	
Make/Set/New/ON/ OFF/Color/Ltype/ Freeze/Thaw:	Return	
Command:		Layer 0 current

2. **Command:** l (line)

From point:	10,10	
To point:	@400,0	
To point:	@0,280	
To point:	@−400,0	
To point:	c (close)	
Command:		Borders drawn

	Command/prompt	Response	Result
3.	**Command:** l (line)		
	From point:	10,30	
	To point:	@400,0	
	To point:	Return	
	Command:		Top of title block
4.	**Command:** s (style)		
	Text style name:	romans	
	Height:	8	
	Width factor <1>:	Return	
	Obliquing angle <0>:	Return	
	Backwards? <N>:	Return	
	Upside-down? <N>:	Return	
	Vertical <N>:	Return	
	Command:		Text style set
5.	**Command:** t (text)		
	<Start point>:	20,15	
	Rotation angle <0>:	Return	
	Text:	An AutoCAD Workbook	
	Command:		Part of title
6.	**Command:** t (text)		
	<Start point>:	280,15	
	Rotation angle <0>:	Return	
	Text:	Work Example 3/1	
	Command:		Remainder of title
7.	**Command:** save	a:\ex03_01	Drawing saved

Introduction to Work Example 3/2

The sequences of instructions given with this Work Example are shortened because the reader will have learned how to manipulate some of the commands from the previous Work Example. Many of the coordinates required are given with Fig. 3.3. Do not include any of the figures or dimensions given in Figs 3.3 or 3.4 in your own drawing.

This Work Example is drawn on several layers. The first task, once in the AutoCAD drawing editor, is to set the necessary layers. The method of doing this is given in item 2 on page 38, except that the layers are made as New layers and do not become the current layers as they are made.

Work Example 3/2

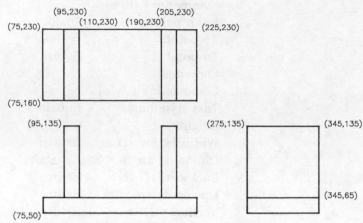

Fig. 3.3 First stage of Work
Example 3/2

Stage 1 (Fig. 3.3)

1. **Main Menu   1. Begin a NEW drawing**
   Enter selection: 1
   Enter NAME of drawing: a:\ex03_02
   When the AutoCAD drawing editor appears:
2. Make New layers:
   Layer CENTRE – colour green; linetype centre
   Layer HIDDEN – colour red; linetype hidden
3. Set **LTSCALE** to 0.5

Command/prompt	Response	Result
4. **Command:** pl (pline)		
From point:	75,230	
Arc/Close/Halfwidth/		
Length/Undo/Width/		
<Endpoint of line>:	w (width)	
Starting width <0>:	0.7	
Ending width <0>:	0.7	Pline width now set at 0.7
<Endpoint of line>:	225,230	
<Endpoint of line>:	225,160	
<Endpoint of line>:	75,160	
<Endpoint of line>:	c (close)	
Command:		Rectangle of plan drawn

5. The pline thickness has now been set at 0.7. Continue drawing
   the outlines of the three views in accordance with the
   coordinate positions given in Fig. 3.3. When these have been
   drawn
6. **Command:** save   ex03_02

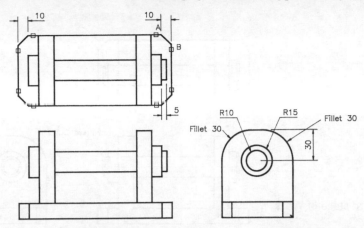

Fig. 3.4 Second stage of
Work Example 3/2

Stage 2 (Fig. 3.4)

	Command/prompt	*Response*	*Result*
1.	**Command:** f (fillet)		
	Polyline/Radius/		
	<Select first object>:	r (radius)	
	Enter fillet radius:	30	
	Command:	*Return*	
	<Select first object:	*pick*	
	Select second object:	*pick*	
	Command:		

2. Fillet the upper corners of the end view as in Fig. 3.4

3.	**Command:** chamfer		
	Polyline/Distance/		
	<Select first line>:	d (distance)	
	Enter first chamfer		
	distance:	10	
	Enter second chamfer		
	distance:	10	
	Command:	*Return*	Chamfers set to 10
	<Select first line>:	pick A	
	Select second line:	pick B	
	Command:		One chamfer drawn

4. Continue in a similar manner to chamfer the four plan corners
5. **Command:** pl (pline)
   draw the straight plines and arc plines to form circles as in Fig. 3.4
6. **Command:** save   ex03_02

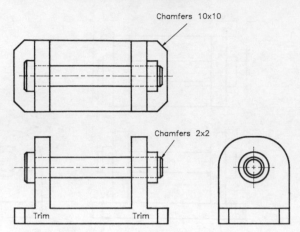

Fig. 3.5 Third stage of Work
Example 3/2

Stage 3 (Fig. 3.5)
1. Set chamfer distances to 2 and construct the chamfers at the
   ends of the rod in both plan and front views. A ZOOM window
   may be needed for this
2. Add the pline double arc to form the circle of the 2 × 2
   chamfers in the end view
3. **Command:** la (layer)
   Make/Set/New/ON/
   OFF/Color/Ltype/
   Freeze/Thaw: s (set)
   New current layer
   <0>:   centre
   Make/Set/New/ON/
   OFF/Color/Ltype/
   Freeze/Thaw: Return
   Command: Layer CENTRE set
4. **Command:** l (line)
   From point: 80,195
   To point: 230,195
   To point: Return
   Command: One centre line drawn
5. Add other centre lines in a similar manner
6. Set layer HIDDEN and draw the hidden detail lines
7. **Command:** trim
   Trim the two lines as shown in Fig. 3.5
8. **Command:** save   ex03_02

Stage 4 (Fig. 3.6)
1. Add border lines and title as shown. Refer to the last two items

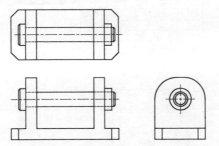

Fig. 3.6 Work Example 3/2

in Work Example 3/1 for the method of adding these

2. **Command:** save   ex03_02

Introduction to Work Example 3/3

This is another example of the construction of a Third Angle orthographic projection. The descriptions of the drawing sequences for the pline outlines of the three views are shorter than in the previous Work Examples because the reader will have followed the pline routines given with them. This Work Example introduces the AutoCAD commands HATCH and DIMENSION.

A note about AutoCAD hatching

A problem which occurs when hatching enclosed areas is that of lines 'leaking' beyond the area to be hatched. There are several methods by which this problem can be overcome. One of these methods is shown in this Work Example – that of using the command BREAK to limit lines (or plines) surrounding the area to the exact limits of the required hatching.

Work Example 3/3

Stage 1 (Fig. 3.7)

1. **Main Menu   1. Begin a NEW drawing**
                    Enter selection: 1
                    Enter NAME of drawing: a:\ex03_03
    When the AutoCAD drawing editor appears:
    Command/prompt   Response   Result
2. **Command:** pl (pline)
    From point: 60,260

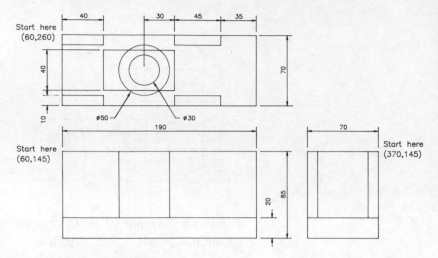

Fig. 3.7 First stage of Work
Example 3/3

Arc/Close/Halfwidth/		
Length/Undo/Width/		
\<Endpoint of line\>:	w (width)	
Starting width \<0\>:	0.7	
Ending width \<0\>:	0.7	Pline width now set at 0.7
\<Endpoint of line\>:	@190,0	
\<Endpoint of line\>:	@0,−70	
\<Endpoint of line\>:	@−190,0	
\<Endpoint of line\>:	c (close)	
Command:		Rectangle of plan drawn

3. The pline thickness has now been set at 0.7. Continue drawing the outlines of the three views in accordance with the dimensions given in Fig. 3.3. When these have been drawn

4. **Command:** pl (pline)

From point:	115,225
\<Endpoint of line\>:	a (arc)
\<Endpoint of arc\>:	s (second)
Second point:	140,250
Endpoint:	165,250
\<Endpoint of arc\>:	s (second)
Second point:	140,190
Endpoint:	115,225
\<Endpoint of arc\>:	Return
Command:	One circle drawn

5. Draw the second pline circle in a similar manner

> Note: The pressing of the Return key when a command has

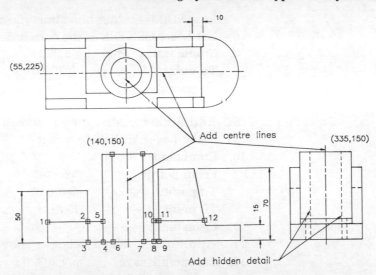

Fig. 3.8 Second stage of
Work Example 3/3

been completed usually brings the last-used command back
into operation

6. **Command:** save   a:\ex03_03   Drawing saved

Stage 2 (Fig. 3.8)

1. **Command:** pl (pline)
    From point: 60,110
    <Endpoint of line>:   @40,0
    <Endpoint of line>:   @0,−50
    <Endpoint of line>:   *Return*
    Command: left end of front view

2. Continue adding pline lines to produce the outlines given in
    Fig. 3.8

3. **Command:** trim
    Select cutting edges...
    Select objects: Select cutting
                               edges and objects
                               until the outline
                               Fig. 3.8 is
                               completed. *Return*
    Command:

4. Set the linetype scale at 0.5

5. Make 5 new layers as follows:
    Layer HIDDEN – colour red; linetype hidden
    Layer CENTRE – colour green; linetype centre
    Layer HATCH – colour blue; linetype continuous
    Layer TEXT – colour magenta; linetype continuous

Layer DIM – colour blue; linetype continuous
6. Set Layer CENTRE as the current layer
7. **Command:** l (line)   55,225
    To point: @200,0
    To point: *Return*
    Command: Centre line drawn
8. Add further centre lines as shown in Fig. 3.8
9. Make Layer HIDDEN current
10. **Command:** l (line)
    From point: 320,145
    To point: @0,−85
    To point: *Return*
    Command: Hidden line drawn
11. Add further hidden detail as shown in Fig. 3.8
12. **Command:** save   a:\ex03_03   Drawing saved
13. **Command:** b (break)
    Select objects: *pick* point 1
    Enter second point: *pick* point 1 again
    Command: Pline broken at 1
14. Repeat item 13 for points 2 to 11
15. The points 1 to 11 are at **SNAP** points so can be *picked*
    accurately. Point 12 is not at a **SNAP** point
    Command: b (break)
    Select objects: *pick* **** from
                              on-screen menu
                              pick **INTersec**
    INTERSEC of: *pick* point 12

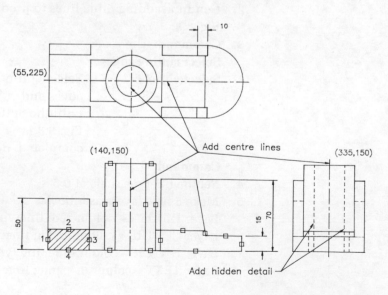

Fig. 3.9 Third stage of Work
Example 3/3

Enter second point:	*pick* ********
	pick **INTersec**
INTERSEC of:	*pick* point 12
	again
Command:	Pline broken at 12

16. **Command:** save   ex03_03

Note: All plines surrounding areas to be hatched are now ready for hatching to commence without 'leaking' occurring

Stage 3 (Fig. 3.9)

1. Set Layer HATCH as the current layer
2. **Command:** hatch

Pattern (? or name/ U,style):	u
Angle for crosshatch lines:	45
Spacing between lines:	4
Double hatch area? <N>:	Return
Select objects:	*pick* point 1
Select objects:	*pick* point 2
Select objects:	*pick* point 3
Select objects:	*pick* point 4
Select objects:	Return
Command:	First area hatched

3. Repeat 1 above for each of the areas to be hatched (Fig. 3.10)

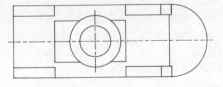

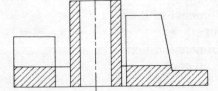

Fig. 3.10 Fourth stage of Work Example 3/3

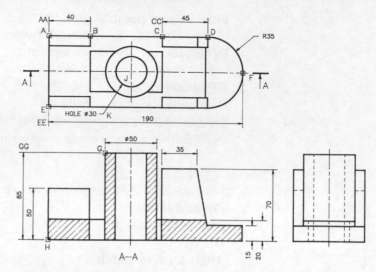

Fig. 3.11 Work Example 3/3

Stage 4 (Fig. 3.11)

1. Set Layer DIM as the current layer
2. **Command:** dim
    Dim: hor (horizontal)
    First extension line
    origin: *pick* point A
    Second extension line
    origin: *pick* point B
    Dimension lines
    location: *pick* point AA
    Dimension text
    <40.0000>:   40
    Command: Dimension inserted
3. Repeat for all horizontal dimensions – examples given in Fig.
    3.11 are B and C and BB; E and F and EE
4. **Command:** dim
    Dim: ver (vertical)
    First extension line
    origin: *pick* point G
    Second extension line
    origin: *pick* point H
    Dimension lines
    location: *pick* point GG
    Dimension text
    <40.0000>:   85
    Command: Dimension inserted

5. Repeat for all vertical dimensions
6. **Command:** dim

Dim:	lea (leader)
Leader start:	*pick* point J
To point:	*pick* point K
To point:	*Return*
Dimension text:	HOLE %%c 30
Command:	Dimension inserted %%c = circle diameter symbol

7. Repeat for the Radius dimension
8. **Command:** pl (pline)

From point:	260,225
Arc/Close/Halfwidth/	
Length/Undo/Width/	
<Endpoint of line>:	w (width)
Starting width <0>:	1
Ending width <0>:	1 Pline width now set at 1
<Endpoint of line>:	@15,0
<Endpoint of line>:	*Return*
Command:	Section plane line end

9. **Command:** pl (pline)

From point:	267,225
Arc/Close/Halfwidth/	
Length/Undo/Width/	
<Endpoint of line>:	w (width)
Starting width <0>:	0
Ending width <0>:	2 Pline width now set at 0 to 2
<Endpoint of line>:	@0,−5
<Endpoint of line>:	*Return*
Command:	Section arrow drawn

10. **Command:** l (line)

From point:	267,225
To point:	@0,−15
To point:	*Return*
Command:	Line of arrow

11. **Command:** cp (copy)

Select objects:	w (window)
First corner:	
Other corner:	*pick* last two plines and line

3 found
Select objects: *Return*
<Base point of
displacement>/
Multiple: *pick* end of arrow
Second point of
displacement: *pick* other end of
                              section line
Command: Section line completed

12. Set layer 0 as the current layer
13. **Command:** l (line)   Add border and
                              title block lines
14. Set Layer TEXT as the current layer
15. Set ROMANS of height 8 as the current text style
16. **Command:** t (text)
                              Add the title text
                              Add A's to
                              section line
17. **Command:** save   ex03_03

Work Example 3/4

Construct this Work Example using the methods already described
in Work Examples 3/1, 3/2 and 3/3. All necessary sizes and details
are given in the four drawings of Figs 3.12 to 3.15. Add a number of
horizontal, vertical and leader dimensions to your completed
drawing.

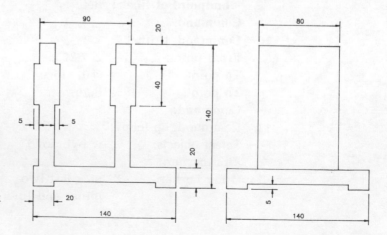

Fig. 3.12 First stage of Work
Example 3/4

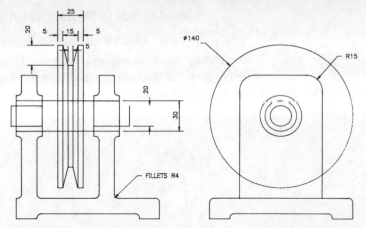

Fig. 3.13 Second stage of
Work Example 3/4

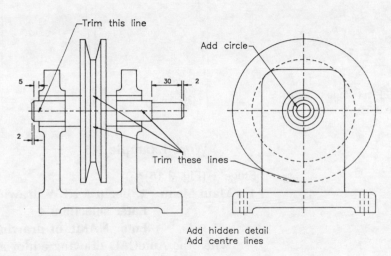

Fig. 3.14 Third stage of Work
Example 3/4

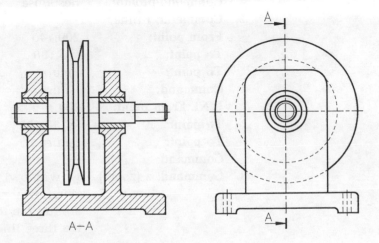

Fig. 3.15 Work Example 3/4

Introduction to Work Example 3/5

The command ARRAY allows polar or rectangular arrays to be accurately and speedily drawn. This example shows how a Polar array allows accurate drawing of a number of repeat outlines in a circular pattern.

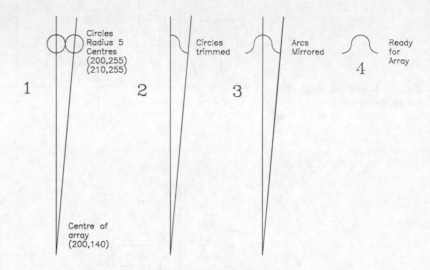

Fig. 3.16 First stage of Work Example 3/5

Work Example 3/5

Stage 1 (Fig. 3.16)

1. **Main Menu   1. Begin a NEW drawing**
   Enter selection: 1
   Enter NAME of drawing: a:\ex03_05

When the AutoCAD drawing editor appears:

Command/prompt	Response	Result
2. **Command:** l (line)		
From point:	200,140	
To point:	@0,130	
To point:	Return	
Command:	Return	Vertical line
LINE From point:	200,140	
To point:	@130<85	
To point:	Return	
Command:		Line at angle 85°
3. **Command:** z (zoom)	w (window)	
	Window area	
	around the top of	
	the three lines	

4. **Command:** c (circle)
    <Center point>:   200,255
    <Radius>:   5
    Command: Return
    CIRCLE <Center
    point>:   210,255
    <Radius>:   5   2 circles drawn

5. **Command:** trim
    Trim the two circles to obtain the arcs as in Stage 2 of Fig. 3.16.
    A ZOOM window may be needed here

6. **Command:** mirror
    Mirror the two arcs to obtain the 4arc outline as in Stage 3 of
    Fig. 3.16

7. **Command:** e (erase)
    Erase the two lines to give the outline only of the arcs as in
    Stage 4 of Fig. 3.16

8. **Command:** save   ex03_05

Stage 2 (Fig. 3.17)

Centre of
Array at
(200,140)

Fig. 3.17 Second stage of
Work Example 3/5

1. **Command:** array
    Select objects: w (window)
    First corner: pick
    Other corner: pick   Window the arcs
    4 found Select objects: Return
    Rectangular or Polar
    array (N/P):   p (Polar)
    Center point of array: 200,140
    Number of items: 36

Angle to fill <360>:   *Return*
Rotate objects as they
are copied? <Y>:   *Return*
Command: *Array completed*

Stage 3 (Fig. 3.18)

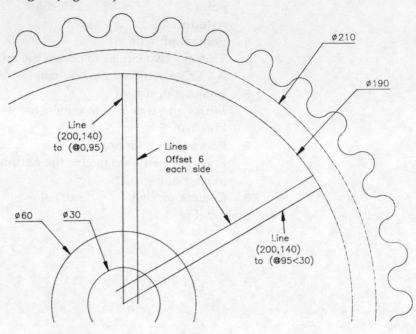

Fig. 3.18 Third stage of Work
Example 3/5

1. **Command:** l (line)
   From point: 200,140
   To point: @0,100
   To point: *Return*
   Command: *Vertical line*
   From point: 200,140
   To point: @100<30
   To point: *Return*
   Command: *Line at 30°*
2. **Command:** c (circle)
   Draw the four circles of centre 240,140 and of diameters 30, 60,
   190 and 210 (Fig. 3.18)
3. **Command:** z (zoom)   w (window)
                                      Window as in
                                      Fig. 3.18
4. **Command:** offset
   Offset distance or
   Through <Through>: 6

Select object to offset: *pick* vertical line
Side to offset: *pick* to right side
Command: parallel line drawn

5. **Command:** offset
Repeat with the line at
30° parallel line drawn

Stage 4 (Fig. 3.19)

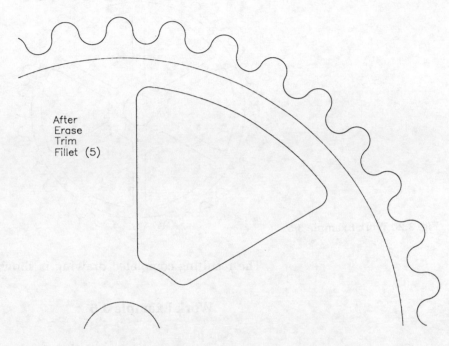

After
Erase
Trim
Fillet (5)

Fig. 3.19 Fourth stage of
Work Example 3/5

1. **Command:** e (erase)
   Erase the vertical and 30° lines
2. **Command:** trim
   Trim unwanted lines ready for fillets to be drawn
3. **Command:** fillet
   Fillet the four corners of the resulting shape at 5 units each
   corner
4. **Command:** z (zoom) zoom All
5. **Command:** array
   Select objects: w (window)
   First corner: *pick*
   Other corner: *pick* Window the shape
   4 found Select objects: *Return*
   Rectangular or Polar
   array (N/P): p (Polar)

Center point of array: 200,140
Number of items: 6
Angle to fill <360>:   Return
Rotate objects as they
are copied? <Y>:   Return
Command: Array completed

Fig. 3.20 Work Example 3/5

The resulting completed drawing is shown in Fig. 3.20.

Work Example 3/6

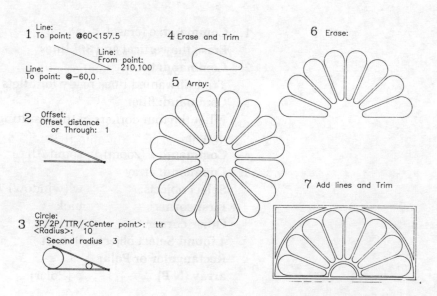

Fig. 3.21 Work Example 3/6

Figure 3.21 is another example of a Polar Array. All details for constructing the Work Example are given in Fig. 3.21. Using the details for constructing an Array for Work Example 3/5 construct Work Example 3/6. Only drawing 7 should be constructed, following the stages shown in drawings 1 to 6.

A note about OSNAPs

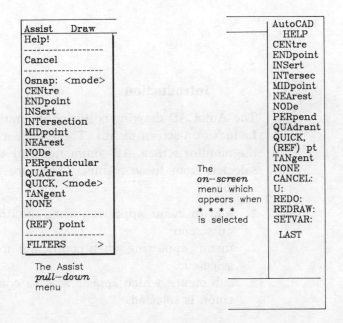

Fig. 3.22 The Assist pull-down menu compared with the OSNAP on-screen menu

During the construction sequences described in this chapter, the OSNAP facility has been referred to. With the aid of the various OSNAPs, accurate positioning of picked points can be achieved. Figure 3.22 shows two methods of selecting OSNAPs – from the pull-down menu Assist or from the on-screen menu which appears when the four asterisks (* * * *) are selected from just below the word AutoCAD in the main on-screen menu. Picked point can be made to snap accurately onto the, e.g., ENDpoints, MIDpoints, etc. of objects already drawn on screen.

CHAPTER 4

Drawing from on-screen menus

Introduction

The AutoCAD drawing editor configuration most commonly used includes on-screen menus. These appear at the right-hand side of the monitor screen. All commands and associated prompts can be selected from these menus. There are three types of on-screen menus:

1. a main menu, appearing when the drawing editor first appears on screen;
2. menus appearing when commands followed by a colon (:) are selected;
3. sub menus which appear when a command not followed by a colon is selected.

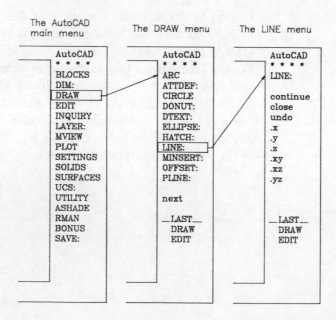

Fig. 4.1 The DRAW and LINE on-screen menus

Figure 4.1 shows the three types. All three include the heading AutoCAD and * * * *. Whichever menu is current, selecting AutoCAD brings up the main menu. Selecting * * * * brings up the OSNAP menu (page 59). A common feature of many of the menus is the LAST, DRAW and EDIT commands below other command and prompts. Selecting one of these three brings up the last menu on screen, the DRAW menu or the EDIT menu. Figure 4.2 shows the main menu and the subsequent sub-menus when the command CIRCLE is selected from the DRAW menu.

Note: At any time the main menu can be made to reappear by selecting the word AutoCAD from the top of any of the menus.

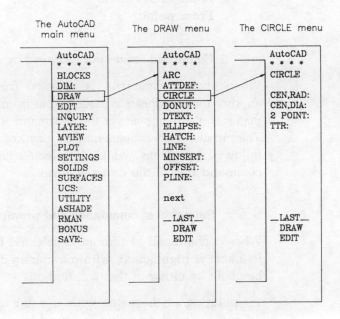

The AutoCAD main menu   The DRAW menu   The CIRCLE menu

Fig. 4.2 The DRAW and CIRCLE on-screen menus

Command names followed by a colon (:)

When such a command is selected, whether from the main menu or from other menus, the command name is repeated at the command line of the drawing editor, together with the first prompt associated with the selected command. A list of possible prompts associated with the command also appears with the command in its on-screen menu. If a command is selected by mistake, the command appearing at the command line can be cancelled by selecting the required command name from the on-screen menu. *Cancel* then appears after the wrongly selected command at the command line and the re-selected command takes its place. Prompts can be selected from an on-screen menu as required. As an example, select

DRAW from the main menu and then LINE: from the menu which appears, the command line will show:

Command:
Command: LINE From point:

If it is then decided that it was not a line, but a pline that was to be drawn, select LAST, the DRAW menu reappears. Select **PLINE:** and the command line changes to:

Command: LINE From point: *Cancel*
Command: PLINE:
From point:

Command names not followed by a colon

When such a command is selected from the on-screen menu, another menu appears replacing that from which the selection was made. Nothing appears at the command line of the drawing editor. The menu which appears may or may not include other commands followed by colons, which if selected call that command to the command line of the drawing editor.

Selection of commands and prompts from menus

When a command or prompt is selected from an on-screen menu, its name is highlighted, within a coloured rectangle. Selection can be made by either of the two methods:

1. pointing at the name with the aid of the selection device – mouse, puck or stylus, followed by pressing the pick button of the device;
2. pressing the Insert key of the keyboard, then selecting the required name with the aid of the up and down cursor keys – those with arrows pointing up and down. Selection is finally made by pressing the Return (Enter) key.

Although in practice the Insert, cursor, Return keys method of selection is rarely used, it may be of value in some circumstances.

Work Examples in this chapter

By now the reader will have become conversant with some of the AutoCAD commands and how to construct simple drawings with the aid of the software. This allows the instructions within the sequences in this chapter to be shorter than in previous chapters. The instructions will follow a pattern such as:

Menu selections	Prompt/action		Result
1. **DRAW**			
LINE:	**From point:**	100,100	
	To point:	100,200	
	To point:	*Return*	
	Command:		Line drawn

In this single instruction, the coordinates can be either:

1. picked with the aid of the selection device and the coordinate numbers appearing on the status line of the drawing editor; or
2. typed at the keyboard. If wished relative coordinates can be typed in place of the given coordinates.

Many of the instructions in the sequences will not be explicit, but will be in the form of a general instruction, such as:

6. Following the method given in item 3 above and with the positions given in Fig. 4.6, complete the outline of the required construction.

Blocks and wblocks

Two of the Work Examples in this chapter involve the insertion of BLOCKs or WBLOCKs into drawings under construction in the drawing editor. The sequence of prompts and responses to the commands BLOCK and WBLOCK are similar. The difference between the results from the two commands is that BLOCKs are saved with the drawing currently under construction, each WBLOCK is saved as a separate drawing file. Thus BLOCKs can only be inserted in the drawing currently under construction; WBLOCKs can be inserted into any drawing including that currently under construction.

The BLOCK sequence of prompts and responses is:

Menu selections	Prompt/action	Result
BLOCKS		
BLOCK:	**Block name (or ?):** valve	
	Insertion base point: *pick*	
	Select objects: (w) window *Key*	
	First corner: *pick*	
	Other corner: *pick*	

30 found. Select objects: *Return*
Command:

The block drawing disappears from the screen, but can be made to reappear if required by:

BLOCKS
BLOCK:
OOPS   **Command:** and the drawing reappears.

If a ? is selected from the **BLOCK:** sub-menu:

BLOCKS
BLOCK:
?

the screen clears and a list of the names and types of block stored with the drawing is listed. This does not happen with WBLOCKs.

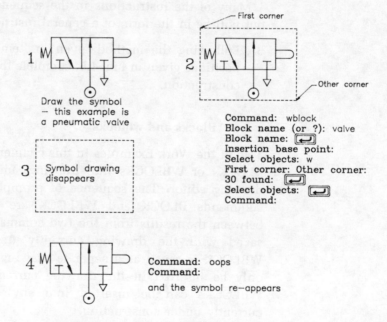

Draw the symbol
– this example is
a pneumatic valve

Symbol drawing
disappears

Command: wblock
Block name (or ?): valve
Block name: [↵]
Insertion base point:
Select objects: w
First corner: Other corner:
30 found: [↵]
Select objects: [↵]
Command:

Command: oops
Command:
and the symbol re–appears

Fig. 4.3 Stages in the
command WBLOCK

Figure 4.3 shows the prompts and responses when WBLOCK is called, together with drawings showing what happens on the screen. The example in this illustration is of the symbol for a 2-port pneumatics valve.

Introduction to Work Example 4/1

This Work Example is a building drawing showing the layout of the rooms of a bungalow. The outer walls and partitions are drawn with plines and all features such as door and window features are inserted from BLOCKs. When the symbols for doors and windows have been inserted the plines are trimmed. Do not include any of the dimensions associated with the drawings for this Work Example

Work Example 4/1

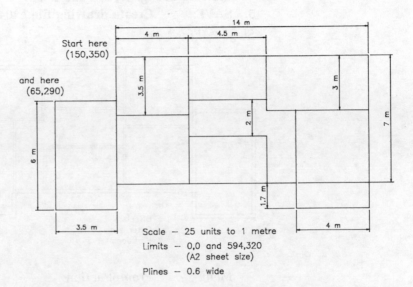

Fig. 4.4 First stage of Work
Example 4/1

Stage 1 (Fig. 4.4)
1. **Main Menu**   **1. Begin a NEW drawing**
                    Enter selection: 1
                    Enter NAME of drawing: a:\ex04_01
    When the AutoCAD drawing editor appears:

Menu selections	*Prompt/action*	*Result*
1. **SETTINGS**		
LIMITS:	**<Lower left corner> <0,0>:**	
	Return	
	Upper right corner: 594,420	A2 sheet size
	Command:	
2. **DISPLAY**		
ZOOM:		
All		Screen set to A2
3. **DRAW**		
PLINE:	**From point:** 150,350	

Width   **Starting width:** .6
            Ending width: .6   Pline set at 0.6
            <Endpoint of line>: @350,0
            <Endpoint of line>: @0,−175
            <Endpoint of line>: @−350,0
            <Endpoint of line>: c (close)

  Command: Plan outline drawn

4. Continue drawing plines of width 0.6 (now set) until the
   drawing of Fig. 4.4 is completed
5. **SAVE:**   **Create drawing file** ex04_01   Precautionary save

Stage 2 (Fig. 4.5)

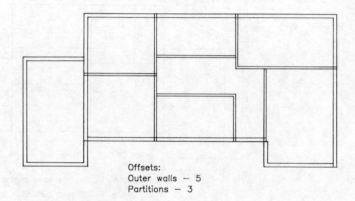

Offsets:
Outer walls — 5
Partitions — 3

Menu selections	Prompt/action	Result

1. **EDIT**
   next
   OFFSET: **Offset distance or Through:** 5

                                Offset set to 5

            Select object to offset: *pick*
            Side to offset: *pick*

Continue picking object and side until the outer wall thicknesses
are constructed as in Fig. 4.5

2. **EDIT**
   next
   OFFSET: **Offset distance or Through:** 3 Offset set to 3
            Select object to offset: *pick*
            Side to offset: *pick*

Continue picking object and side until the partition thicknesses
are constructed as in Fig. 4.5

3. **SAVE:**   **Create drawing file**
                     a:\ex04_01   Precautionary save

Stage 3 (Fig. 4.6)

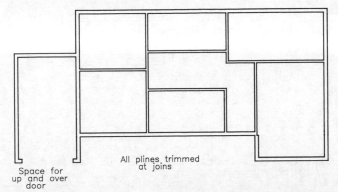

Fig. 4.6 Third stage of Work
Example 4/1

Space for
up and over
door

All plines trimmed
at joins

Menu selections	Prompt/action	Result

1. **EDIT**
    next
    TRIM: **Select cutting edge(s). . .**
                     Select objects: *pick*
                     1 selected, 1 found
                     Select objects: *pick*
                     1 selected, 1 found *Ret*
                     <Select object to trim>: *pick*

Continue until all parts of plines are trimmed to obtain the results shown in Fig. 4.6.

Note: A **ZOOM** window will be required for some of the trimming.

2. **SAVE:**   **Create drawing file**
                     a:\ex04_01   Precautionary save

Stage 4 (Fig. 4.7)

The drawings of symbols for this stage can be drawn on any part of the drawing editor not occupied by the constructions drawn so far.

Menu selections	Prompt/action	Result

1. **DRAW**
    LINE: **Line From point:** anywhere on
                     screen
                     To point: @50,0
                     To point: Return

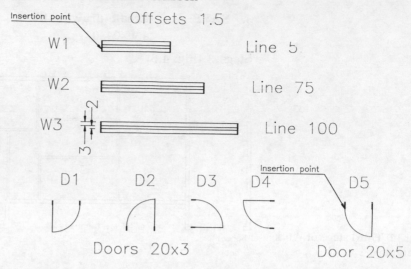

Fig. 4.7 Drawings of BLOCKs
for Work Example 4/1

	Command:	Line of W1 drawn
2. **EDIT**		
next		
OFFSET:	**Offset distance or Through:** 3	
	Select object to offset: *pick* line	
	Side to offset: *pick*	
	Select object to offset: *Ret*	
	Command: *Ret*	
	Offset distance or Through: 2	
	Select object to offset: *pick* offset	
	Side to offset: *pick*	
	Select object to offset: *Ret*	
	Command: *Ret*	
	Offset distance or Through: 3	
	Select object to offset: *pick* line	
	Side to offset: *pick*	
	Select object to offset: *Ret*	
	Command: *Ret*	All lines of W1 drawn
3. **DRAW**		
PLINE:	**From point:** pick end of first line	
	<Endpoint of line>: *pick* end of lowest line	
	<Endpoint of line>: *Ret*	
	Command: *Ret*	

From point: *pick* other end

<Endpoint of line>: *pick*
other end

<Endpoint of line>: *Ret*

Command:

4. Repeat to obtain the other two window symbols with lines of 75 and 100 coordinate units long. This gives scaled window symbols of 2 metres, 3 metres and 4 metres

5. In a similar manner draw the door symbols each 20 units wide, D1, D2, D3 and D4 with 3-unit plines and D5 with 5-unit plines at their base ends

6. Make a BLOCK of each symbol following the sequence for the **BLOCK** command given on page 63. As each block, the symbol disappears from the screen. Do NOT bring it back on the screen

   Note: Take care with selection of an insertion point for each of the symbols. Your work will be made much easier if the insertion point matches a snap point in the outline pline plan already drawn.

Stage 5 (Fig. 4.8)

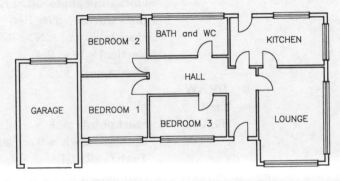

Fig. 4.8 Work Example 4/1

Menu selections	Prompt/action	Result
1. **DRAW**		
INSERT:	**Block name (or ?):** w2	W2 dragged on screen
	Insertion point: *pick*	
	X scale factor<1>: *Ret*	
	Y scale factor (default=X): *Ret*	
	Rotation angle <0>: *Ret*	
	Command:	Window inserted

2. Repeat for all window and door symbols as shown in Fig. 4.8.

Some of the door symbols will have to be rotated through either 90° or 270° in response to the prompt **Rotation angle <0>**:

3. **EDIT**
    EXPLODE: **Select block reference,**
                   polyline dimension or mesh:
                   pick each inserted **BLOCK** in
                   turn

    Note: If the blocks are not exploded they cannot be used for trimming unwanted parts of polylines in the next operation.

4. **EDIT**
    TRIM: Trim all plines within the
                   areas of the inserted windows
                   and doors   Plan completed

5. **Style**   *Keyboard Return*
    Romans   *Keyboard Return*   Select font file
                                                      box appears

    Text style name: romans
                   Height: 8
                   Width factor <1>: *Ret*
                   Obliquing angle <0>: *Ret*
                   Backwards? <N> *Ret*
                   Upside-down? <N>: *Ret*
                   Vertical <N>: *Ret*
                   Command: Text style set

6. **DRAW**
    next
    TEXT: **Start point:** *pick*
                   Rotation angle <0>: *Ret*
                   Text: GARAGE
                   Command: Text GARAGE
                                                      drawn

7. Repeat to enter all the room names.

8. **DRAW**
    LINE: **From point:** 20,20
                   To point: @560,0
                   To point: @0,390
                   To point: @−560,0
                   To point: c (close)
                   Command: Borders drawn

9. Add line for top of title block

10. Add text in title with text style set to ROMANS of height 12

11. **SAVE:**   a:\ex04_01   Drawing saved

Introduction to Work Example 4/2

Figure 4.9 consists of drawings of a number of electronic circuit symbols from British Standard BS: 3939. This Work Example is intended to give practice in the drawing and saving of the symbols as BLOCKs and their subsequent INSERTion into an electronic circuit drawing. Only very limited instructions are given for constructing the required circuit diagram. This is on the assumption that the information given earlier in this chapter will enable the reader to complete the circuit drawing without difficulty.

There is no need to include the names of the symbols when constructing the required BLOCK drawings. Suitable BLOCK filenames would be: bat for the battery; cap for the capacitor; npn for the npn transistor, and so on.

Work Example 4/2

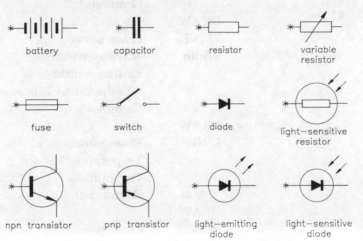

Fig. 4.9 Drawings of electronic symbols for BLOCKs

The * shows the insertion point for each block
The * is NOT included with the block

Stage 1 (Fig. 4.9)
1. **Main Menu**   **1. Begin a NEW drawing**
                   Enter selection: 1
                   Enter NAME of drawing: a:\ex04_02
   When the AutoCAD drawing editor appears:
2. Draw the symbols with the **DRAW** menu commands **LINE:**, **CIRCLE:** and **PLINE:**

As an example, the drawing of the light-emitting diode symbol is described in item 3 below.

Menu selections	Prompt/action	Result
3. **DRAW**		
CIRCLE		
CEN,RAD:	<Centre point>: *pick*	
	<Radius>: 15	
	Command:	Circle drawn
DRAW		
LINE:	From point: *pick*	
	To point: @60,0	
	Command:	Line drawn
DRAW		
PLINE:	From point: *pick*	
Width	**Starting width:** 0	
	Ending width: 10	
	<Endpoint of line>: *pick*	Diode arrow drawn
	Command:	
DRAW		
PLINE:	From point: *pick*	
Width	**Starting width:** 2	
	Ending width: 2	
	<Endpoint of line>: @10,0	Diode plate drawn
	Command:	
DRAW		
LINE:	From point: *pick*	
	To point: @15<45	
	To point: Ret	
	Command:	Line of pointer
DRAW		
PLINE:	From point: *pick* end of line	
Width	**Starting width:** 0	
	Ending width: 2	
	<Endpoint of line>: @6<225	Pointer arrow drawn
	Command:	
EDIT		
COPY:		
Window	**First corner:** *pick*	
	Other corner: *pick*	
	Select objects: Ret	
	<Base point of displacement>: *pick*	
	Second point of	

displacement: *pick*

Command: Second pointer

4. Make a **BLOCK** from the symbol under the filename LED
5. Repeat with each of the symbols shown in Fig. 4.9
6. **SAVE:**   a:\ex04_02   Drawing saved

Note. Check the blocks saved with the drawing as follows:

7. **DRAW**

    INSERT: ?

              Block(s) to list <*>: *Ret*

A screen such as the following will appear:

Defined blocks

BAT

CAP

RES

VARRES

FUSE

SWITCH

User	Unnamed
Blocks	**Blocks**
6	**0**

Command:

8. **Press key F1 to return to drawing editor**

Stage 2 (Fig. 4.10)

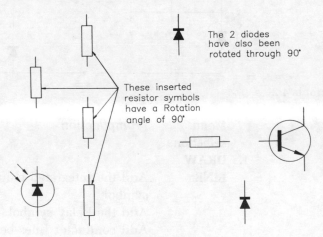

The 2 diodes have also been rotated through 90°

These inserted resistor symbols have a Rotation angle of 90°

Fig. 4.10 First stage of Work Example 4/2

Menu selections	Prompt/action	Result

1. **DRAW**

    INSERT: **Block name (or ?)** res (for resistor block)

              Insertion point: *pick*

                              X scale factor <1>: *Ret*

                              Y scale factor (default=X): *Ret*

                              Rotation angle <0>: 90

                              Command: A resistor inserted

2. Repeat with the various symbols shown in Fig. 4.10, inserting them at points approximately positioned.

    Note: Symbols which have been inserted in this way can be treated as single objects for MOVEing, COPYing, ERASEing etc. This means that they can be easily moved to new positions if necessary as the circuit drawing develops. It may be quicker to COPY some INSERTed symbols than to INSERT another of the same type.

3. **SAVE:**   a:\ex04_02   Drawing saved

Stage 3 (Fig. 4.11)

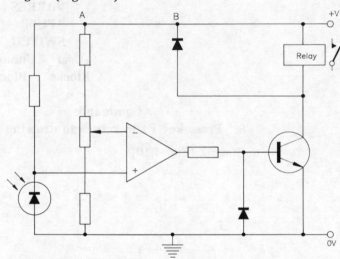

Fig. 4.11 Work Example 4/2

Menu selections	Prompt/action	Result
1. **DRAW**		
LINE:	Add the Integrated chip symbol	
	Add the Relay symbol	
	Add conductor lines between symbols	
	Add the Earth symbol	
	Add parts of the Relay switch	Circuit complete
2. **DRAW**		
DONUT:	**Inside diameter <1>:** 0	
	Outside diameter <1>: 3	

Center of donut: *pick*
points where conductors
intersect, e.g. A, B etc.   Dots at
                                           intersections

3. **DRAW
   PLINE:**   Add arrow from IC symbol
                  Add details to relay switch   Arrows added
4. **DRAW
   TEXT:**   Add +V and 0V
5. **DRAW
   LINE:**   Add borders and title block
                  lines
6. **DRAW
   TEXT**   Add title – ROMANS – 8 high
7. **SAVE:**   a:\ex04_02   Drawing saved

Work Example 4/3

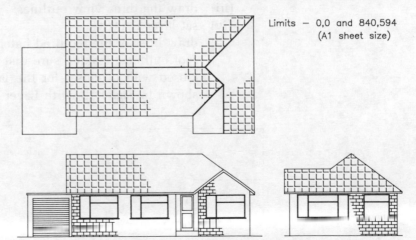

Limits – 0,0 and 840,594
(A1 sheet size)

Fig. 4.12 Work Example 4/3

This Work Example has been included here to describe a second method of adding hatching to drawings constructed in AutoCAD. In an earlier Work Example (3/3, page 45), hatching lines were confined to an area by the BREAKing of lines at intersections around the area. In this present Work Example, another method is employed. The outline of the area to be hatched is drawn on a separate layer (HATCH). Hatching is performed on another layer (ROOF), within the outline. Then the layer HATCH is turned OFF.

As it is only this different method of hatching with which we are concerned here, there is no real need to work the whole Example.

However if it is wished to do so, the following should be observed:

1.   set the drawing area limits to 840 by 594 (A1 sheet sizes);
2.   the three views in Fig. 4.12 are of the bungalow shown in the building plan Fig. 4.8. Thus overall sizes can be assumed from that drawing;
3.   the door and window outlines in the front and end view of Fig. 4.12 are shown enlarged in Fig. 4.14. All the parallel lines of these two items can be constructed with the aid of the **OFFSET** command;
4.   the drawing should be constructed in layers:
     Layer 0   – outlines; colour white
     Layer ROOF   – hatch lines; colour red
     Layer HATCH– hatch area outlines; colour yellow
     Layer TEXT   – text; colour cyan
5.   work in the follow order:
     (i)   set limits;
     (ii)   zoom all;
     (iii) draw the three view outlines;
     (iv)   set layer HATCH;
     (v)   draw lines of the required hatch areas over the existing roof outlines, making sure that each polygon outline is closed with c (close) for the last line of each. This is shown in Fig. 4.13, with Layer 0 tuned off;

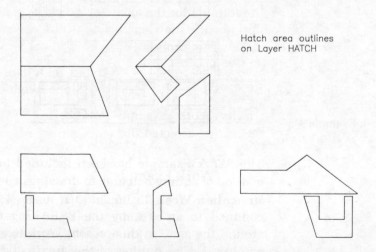

Hatch area outlines
on Layer HATCH

Fig. 4.13 Hatch areas for
Work Example 4/3

     (vi)   set layer ROOF;
     (vii) hatch the various areas – using hatch patterns **angle** (scale for pattern 2) and **brick** (scale for pattern 1);
     (viii) turn layer HATCH off – it then disappears from the

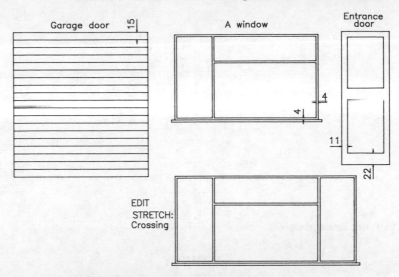

Fig. 4.14 Windows and
doors for Work Example 4/3

screen leaving the hatching as required;

(ix)   add borders, title block and title.

Introduction to Work Example 4/4

The construction of surface developments of solids is a compara-
tively easy task when using AutoCAD. In this example the
development of the surface of a right cone is constructed by using
the formula for the angle included in an arc. This formula depends
on knowing the slope height of the cone and the radius of its base
circle. The formula is:

$$\text{Included angle} = \frac{360 \times \text{Radius of base circle}}{\text{Slope height of cone}}\text{(in degrees)}$$

This Work Example makes use of the command DIST for
measuring selected distances on the screen.

Work Example 4/4

1. **Main Menu   1. Begin a NEW drawing**
                Enter selection: 1
                Enter NAME of drawing: a:\ex04_04

    When the AutoCAD drawing editor appears:

    *Menu   Prompt/action   Result
    selections*

2. Draw the front view and plan of the cone to the dimensions
    given in Fig. 4.15, using **LINE:** and **CIRCLE:** from the **DRAW**
    menu

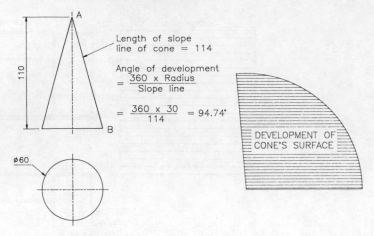

Length of slope
line of cone = 114

Angle of development
$= \dfrac{360 \times \text{Radius}}{\text{Slope line}}$

$= \dfrac{360 \times 30}{114} = 94.74°$

DEVELOPMENT OF
CONE'S SURFACE

ø60

Fig. 4.15 Work Example 4/4

3. **INQUIRY**
    DIST: **First point:** *pick* A
                       Second point: *pick* B   **Distance = 114**
                       Command:

    Note: Other information about the distance – its angle in the X–Y
    plane; its angle from the X–Y plane; Delta X, Y and Z. In this case
    however we are only concerned with the distance

4. **DRAW**
    ARC
    C,S,A: **Center:** 260,80
                       Start point: @140,0
                       Included angle: 94.74
                       Command: Arc of
                                                           development

5. **DRAW**
    LINE: **From point:** 260,80
                       To point: @140,0
                       To point: *Ret*
                       Command: *Ret*
                       From point: 260,80
                       To point: @140<94.74
                       To point: *Ret*
                       Command: Lines of
                                                           development

6. **DRAW**
    next
    TEXT:
    STYLE: **Fonts**
    Romans   *pick* ROMANS from dialogue

		box followed by **OK**	
		Height: 6	
		Width factor <1>: *Ret*	
		Obliquing angle <0>: *Ret*	
		Backwards? <N> *Ret*	
		Upside-down? <N>· *Ret*	
		Vertical <N>: *Ret*	
		Command:	Text style set
7.	**DRAW**		
	DTEXT:	**<Start point>:** 270,130	
		Rotation angle <0>: *Ret*	
		Text: DEVELOPMENT OF *Ret*	
		CONE'S SURFACE *Ret*	
		Command:	Text appears
8.	**LAYER:**		
	Make	**New current layer:** hatch	
	Colour	**Color:** yellow *Ret* (twice)	
		Command:	Layer HATCH
			made and current
9.	**DRAW**		
	LINE:	Draw lines around last text	
10.	**LAYER:**	Make another Layer –	
		HATCH01	Layer HATCH01
			made and current
11.	**DRAW**		
	HATCH:	u	
		Angle for cross hatch lines	
		<0>: *Ret*	
		Spacing between lines <1>:	
		3	
		Double hatch area? <N>: *Ret*	
		Select objects: pick lines	
		around development and text	
		in turn	
		Select objects: *Ret*	
		Command:	Area hatched
12.	**LAYER:**		
	OFF	**Layer name(s) to turn Off:**	
		hatch *Ret* (twice)	Lines clear
13.	**SAVE:**	a:\ex04_04	Drawing saved

Introduction to isometric drawing

Four Work Examples in which isometric drawings will be constructed in the drawing editor are included here. There are two methods for the construction of isometric drawings:

1. Keying relative coordinates to position the ends of lines. This Work Example uses this method.
2. With the aid of the ISO style SNAP setting and a GRID and picking points on the isometric grid on the screen. This is the chosen method for the other isometric drawing Work Examples.

When using the second of these two methods, four command systems are available – GRID, SNAP, ISOPLANE and ELLIPSE. The settings for these are described in the sequences below. The easiest way in which to operate the ISOPLANE facility is by pressing the Ctrl and E keys. This rotates (in a clockwise direction), the faces on which an imaginary isometric cube would be drawn. Press the two keys repeatedly and the following appears at the command line:

<Isoplane Top> <Isoplane Right> <Isoplane Left>

As each Isoplane surface appears on screen, so the cursor cross-hairs switch to new isometric planes.

Work Example 4/5

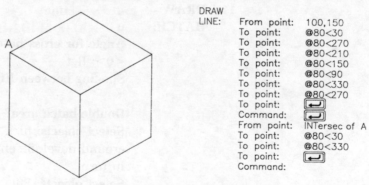

```
DRAW
LINE:   From point:  100,150
        To  point:   @80<30
        To  point:   @80<270
        To  point:   @80<210
        To  point:   @80<150
        To  point:   @80<90
        To  point:   @80<330
        To  point:   @80<270
        To  point:   ⏎
        Command:     ⏎
        From point:  INTersec of A
        To  point:   @80<30
        To  point:   @80<330
        To  point:   ⏎
        Command:
```

Fig. 4.16 Work Example 4/5

1. **Main Menu   1. Begin a NEW drawing**
   Enter selection: 1
   Enter NAME of drawing: a:\ex04_06

   When the AutoCAD drawing editor appears:

Menu selections	Prompt/action	Result

2. **DRAW**
   LINE: Follow the details given in Fig. 4.16

3. **Draw**
   TEXT: Add borders, title and title
               block
4. **SAVE:**   a:\ex04_06   Drawing saved

Work Example 4.6

Choose your own dimensions when constructing this Example. You will find that, providing you set the Isoplane as suggested, the cursor cross-hairs will assist in obtaining an accurate isometric drawing.

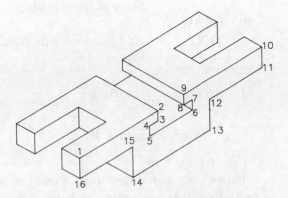

Fig. 4.17 Work Example 4/6

1. **Main Menu   1. Begin a NEW drawing**
                Enter selection: 1
                Enter NAME of drawing: a:\ex04_06

   When the AutoCAD drawing editor appears:

Menu selections	Prompt/action	Result
2. **SETTINGS**		
GRID:	Grid spacing (X): 10	
	Command:	Grid set ON to 10
3. **SETTINGS:**		
next		
SNAP:		
Style		
Iso	**Vertical spacing:** 10	
	Command:	Isometric grid appears
4.	Press Ctrl+E until **<Isoplane Right>** is set	Isoplane Right set
5. **DRAW**		
LINE:	**From point:** *pick* 1	

		To point: *pick* points 2 to 16 in turn	Right face drawn
6.		Press Ctrl+E until **<Isoplane Top>** is set	
7.	**DRAW LINE:**	Draw lines for top of the drawing	
8.		Press Ctrl+E until **<Isoplane Left>** is set	
9.	**DRAW LINE:**	Draw lines for the left-hand faces of the drawing	Drawing completed
10.	**DRAW TEXT:**	Add borders, title block and title	Work Exercise completed
11.	**SAVE:**	a:\ex04_06	Drawing saved

Work Example 4/7

Stage 1 (Fig. 4.18)
Choose your own dimensions when constructing this Example. You will find that, providing you set the Isoplane as suggested, the cursor cross-hairs will assist in obtaining an accurate isometric drawing.

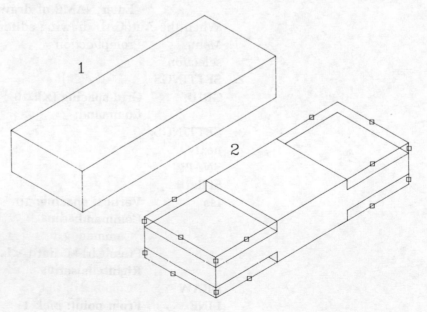

Fig. 4.18 First stage of Work Example 4/7

1. **Main Menu** **1. Begin a NEW drawing**
   Enter selection: 1
   Enter NAME of drawing: a:\ex04_07

When the AutoCAD drawing editor appears:

Menu selections	Prompt/action	Result
2. **SETTINGS**		
GRID:	**Grid spacing (X): 10**	
	Command:	Grid set ON to 10
3. **SETTINGS:**		
next		
SNAP:		
Style		
Iso	**Vertical spacing: 10**	
	Command:	Isometric grid appears
4.	Press Ctrl+E until **<Isoplane TOP>** is set	Isoplane Top set
5. **DRAW**		
LINE:	Draw outline as in Fig. 4.18 Drawing 1, changing the Isoplane as necessary	
6. **DRAW**		
LINE:	Add lines as in Fig. 4.18 Drawing 2, changing the Isoplane as necessary	
7. **EDIT**		
ERASE: and		
TRIM:	Erase and trim those lines marked with a pick box in Fig. 4.18 Drawing 2	
8. **SAVE:**	a:\ex04_07	

Stage 2 (Fig. 4.19)

1. **DRAW**		
ELLIPSE:		
Iso	**Center of circle:** *pick*	
	<Circle radius>: *pick*	
	Command: *Ret*	Ellipse drawn
Iso	**Center of circle:** *pick*	
	<Circle radius>: *pick*	
	Command: *Ret*	2nd Ellipse drawn
Iso	**Center of circle:** *pick*	

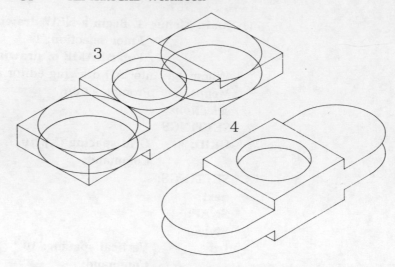

Fig. 4.19 Second stage of
Work Example 4/7

	<Circle radius>: *pick*	
	Command: *Ret*	3rd Ellipse drawn
Iso	**Center of circle:** *pick*	
	<Circle radius>: *pick*	
	Command: *Ret*	4th Ellipse drawn
Iso	**Center of circle:** *pick*	
	<Circle radius>: *pick*	
	Command: *Ret*	5th Ellipse drawn
Iso	**Center of circle:** *pick*	
	<Circle radius>: *pick*	
	Command: *Ret*	6th Ellipse drawn

2. **EDIT**
   ERASE:
   and
   TRIM: Erase and trim to obtain
   details as Drawing 4 of
   Fig. 4.19   Fig. 4.19 drawn

3. **SAVE:**   a:\ex04_07

Stage 3 (Fig. 4.20)

1. **DRAW**
   ELLIPSE:

Iso	**Center of circle:** *pick*	
	<Circle radius>: *pick*	
	Command: *Ret*	Ellipse drawn
Iso	**Center of circle:** *pick*	
	<Circle radius>: *pick*	
	Command: *Ret*	2nd Ellipse drawn

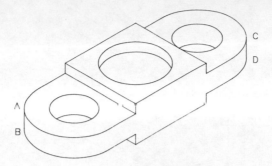

Fig. 4.20 Work Example 4/7

Iso	**Center of circle:** *pick*	
	<Circle radius>: *pick*	
	Command: *Ret*	3rd Ellipse drawn
Iso	**Center of circle:** *pick*	
	<Circle radius>: *pick*	
	Command: *Ret*	4th Ellipse drawn
2. **DRAW**		
LINE:	**From point:**	
	NEArest to *pick* A	
	To point:	
	TANgent to *pick* B	
	To point: Return	
	Command: Return	
	From point:	
	NEArest to *pick* C	
	To point:	
	TANgent to *pick* D	
	To point: *Ret*	
	Command:	Lines at ends of part ellipses
3. **EDIT**		
TRIM:	Trim parts of ellipse to last drawn lines	Drawing completed
4. **DRAW**		
LINE: and		
TEXT:	Add borders and title	Drawing completed
5. **SAVE:**	a:/ex40_07	Drawing saved

Work Example 4/8

Stage 1 (Fig. 4.21)

1. **Main Menu   1. Begin a NEW drawing**

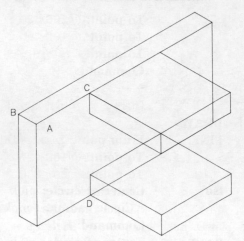

Fig. 4.21 First stage of Work
Example 4/8

Enter selection: 1
Enter NAME of drawing: a:\ex04_08

When the AutoCAD drawing editor appears:

Menu selections	*Prompt/action*	*Result*
2. **SETTINGS**		
GRID:	**Grid spacing (X): 10**	
	Command:	Grid set ON to 10
3. **SETTINGS:**		
next		
SNAP:		
Style		
Iso	**Vertical spacing: 10**	
	Command:	Isometric grid appears
4.	Press Ctrl+E until **<Isoplane TOP>** is set	Isoplane Top set
5. **DRAW**		
LINE:	**From point:** *pick* approx 115,135	
	To point: @200<30	
	To point: @20<330	
	To point: @200<210	
	To point: c (close)	
	Command:	Outline top edge
6.	Ctrl+E to **<Isoplane Right>**	
7. **DRAW**		
LINE:	**From point:** *pick* point A	
	To point: @100<270	

	To point: @200<30	
	To point: @100<90	
	To point: c (close)	
	Command:	Outline front drawn
8.	Ctrl+E to <Isoplano Loft>	
9.	**DRAW**	
	LINE: **From point:** *pick* point B	
	To point: @100<270	
	To point: @20<330	
	Command:	Outline end

10. In a similar manner draw the two lugs, starting first at C, then at D. Each lug is 80 × 80 × 20

11.	**SAVE:**	a:\ex04_08	Drawing saved

Stage 2 (Fig. 4.22)

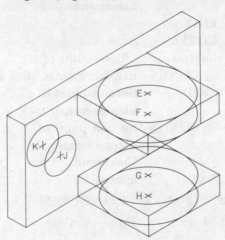

Fig. 4.22 Second stage of Work Example 4/8

Menu selections	*Prompt and action*	Result
1.	Ctrl+E to <**Isoplane Top**>	
2. **DRAW**		
ELLIPSE:		
	Iso	
Center	**Center of circle:** *pick* E	
	<**Circle radius**>: 40	
	Command:	1st ellipse drawn
3. **EDIT**		
COPY:		
Last		
Multiple	**Multiple base point:** *pick* E	

	Second point of displacement: *pick* F	
	Second point of displacement: *pick* G	
	Second point of displacement: *pick* H	
	Second point of displacement: *Ret*	
	Command:	3 ellipses copied
4.	Ctrl+E to **<Isoplane Right>**	
5. **DRAW ELLIPSE: Iso Center**	**Center of circle:** *pick* J **<Circle radius>:** 18	
	Command:	1 ellipse drawn
6. **EDIT COPY: Last**	**<Base point of displacement>:** *pick* J	
	Second point of displacement: *pick* K	
	Second point of displacement: *Ret*	
	Command:	2nd ellipse copied
7. **SAVE:**	a:\ex04_08	Drawing saved

Stage 3 (Figs 4.23, 4.24 and 4.25)

Menu selections	Prompt/action	Result
1. **EDIT**		

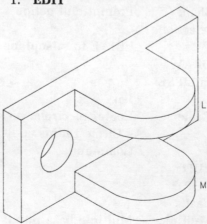

Fig. 4.23 Third stage (1) of
Work Example 4/8

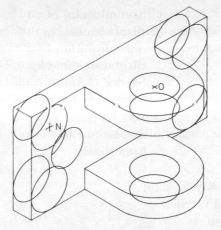

Fig. 4.24 Third stage (2) of Work Example 4/8

TRIM: and

ERASE: Trim and erase parts of ellipses and lines to obtain Fig. 4.23

Note: It is possible that the lines and ellipses will not trim properly as required. If this happens, use:

EDIT

BREAK: Select object: *pick* a line or ellipse

First Enter first point:

Enter second point:

Command:

However it may be necessary to BREAK an ellipse into several parts for this to be successful.

2. Add lines L and M with the aid of the **OSNAPs ENDpoint** and **NEA**rest

3. Ctrl+E to <Isoplane Right>

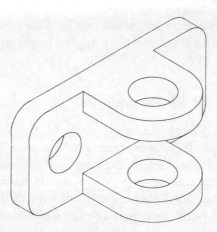

Fig. 4.25 Third stage (3) of Work Example 4/8

4. Draw the ellipse of centre N and radius 20
5. Copy the ellipse of centre N to other positions with the aid of the **Multiple** prompt of the **COPY:** command
6.   Ctrl+E to **<Isoplane TOP>**
7. Draw ellipse of centre O and radius 20
8. Copy the last ellipse to the other three positions with the aid of the **Multiple** prompt of the **COPY:** command
9. Trim part ellipses and lines to obtain the outline of Fig. 4.25
10. **SAVE:**   a:\ex04_08   Drawing saved

Stage 4 (Fig. 4.26)

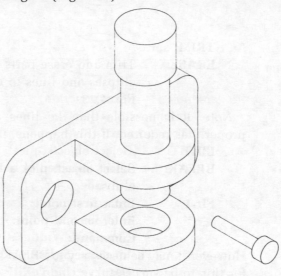

Fig. 4.26 Work Example 4/8

Menu selections	Prompt/action	Result

1. Using similar drawing techniques as in stages 1 to 3, add the two pins as shown in Fig. 4.26
2. Add lines and text to give borders, title and title block
3. **SAVE:**   a:\ex04_08   Drawing saved

Work Example 4/9

In this Work Example some of the outlines from the previous Example have been redrawn as plines of 1 unit width. This gives such an isometric drawing an appearance of depth, as if the drawing was standing out from its background. The thickening of the lines is carried out with the aid of the command PEDIT. When PEDIT (edit polylines) is called the command line changes to:

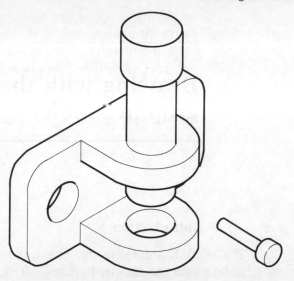

Fig. 4.27 Work Example 4/9

Menu selections	Prompt/action	Result
EDIT	**next**	
PEDIT:	**Select objects:** *pick*	
	Entity selected is not a	
	polyline	
	Do you want to change it	
	into one <Y> *Ret*	
	Close/Join/Width/Edit vertex/	
	Fit curve/Spline curve/	
	Decurve/Undo/eXit/<X>:	

in response to this series of prompts, if a line is to be changed to a polyline of Width 1, type w (width), followed by 1.

If a curve is to be changed to a pline, first type s (Spline curve) to change the curve to a Spline curve. Then w (Width) followed by 1.

In order to obtain results exactly as in Fig. 4.27, some breaking of the newly-formed plines may be necessary.

CHAPTER 5

Drawing with the aid of a graphics tablet

Introduction

The Work Examples in this chapter are based on using a graphics tablet with a standard AutoCAD Release 11 tablet overlay. However, as in Work Examples in other chapters, those in this chapter can also be worked from commands typed at the keyboard or selected from pull-down or on-screen menus. The graphics tablet and its overlay form yet another method of drawing with AutoCAD. Only a limited number of the commands available from the overlay will be described here.

The AutoCAD graphics tablet overlay

1. The details given in this chapter assume that the tablet overlay has been configured – under SETTINGS – TABLET – CONFIG.
2. A puck or a stylus is used as the selection device for picking commands from the tablet.
3. In this chapter only the pick button of the selection device is referred to. Other buttons on multi-button pucks may be configured to toggle Cancel, Grid, Snap, Coords, or Isoplane. The use of these other buttons is not described here.
4. Blank strips between menu areas can be picked to operate as if the Return key of the keyboard is pressed (Fig. 5.4).
5. Most of the AutoCAD commands can be assessed from the overlay. Even those not included can be selected from the area marked SCREEN MENU of the overlay.
6. Commands are directly assessed from the overlay, without going through a menu, sub-menu routine. A picked command is repeated at the command line of the drawing editor.
7. When the selection device is moved over the MONITOR area of the tablet, the monitor screen cursor cross-hairs respond by moving in coordination with the positions of the selection device.

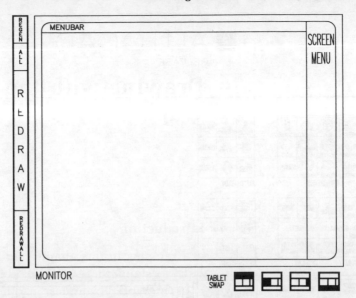

Fig. 5.1 The AutoCAD
Release 11 overlay monitor
area

8. The tablet must be turned on, either by typing TABLET and responding with ON, or pressing function key f10.

The AutoCAD Release 11 tablet overlay

Figure 5.2 shows the AutoCAD Release 11 tablet overlay. Many of the command names are accompanied with icons.

Figure 5.3 shows a puck with four buttons placed in position with its cross-hairs over the CIRCLE command. When the pick button (the top button of this puck) is pressed, the command comes into action and the command name appears at the command line of the drawing editor.

The outlines of the menu areas which include the commands referred to in this chapter are given in Fig. 5.4.

Notes on Work Examples

This book comprises a series of Examples forming a course of work for readers. So far the Examples have described the constructions using pull-down menus, typing commands from the keyboard and using on-screen menus. This chapter is concerned with drawing mainly with the aid of the AutoCAD Release 11 graphics overlay with a graphics tablet. As this chapter is the last before we go on to three-dimensional and solid model drawing, the Examples in this chapter are more varied than in previous chapters. It is assumed the

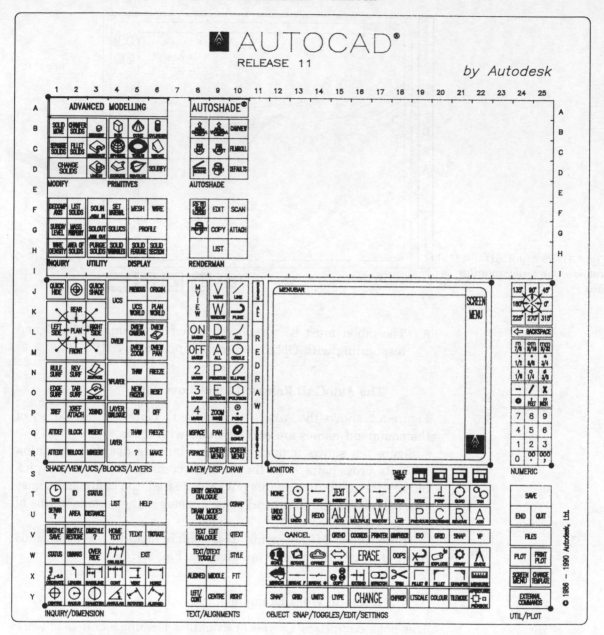

Fig. 5.2 The AutoCAD
Release 11 graphics tablet
overlay

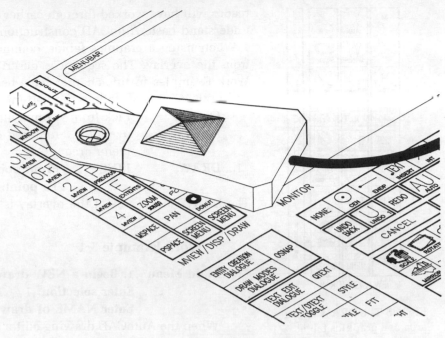

Fig. 5.3 A puck positioned
for selecting CIRCLE on a
graphics overlay

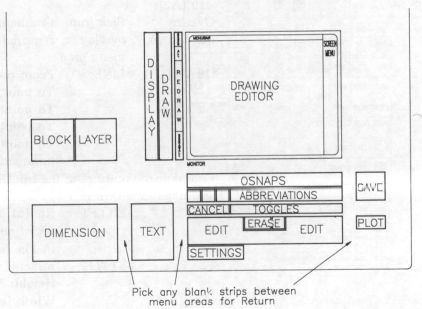

Fig. 5.4 Outlines of menu
areas on a graphics tablet
overlay

Pick any blank strips between
menu areas for Return

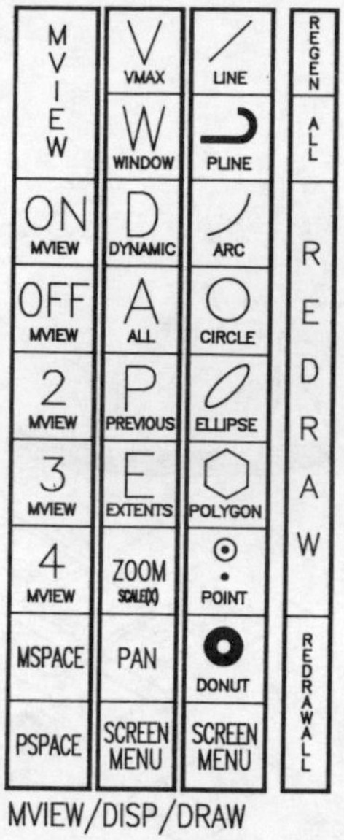

MVIEW/DISP/DRAW

Fig. 5.5 The DRAW menu
area of a graphics tablet
overlay

reader will have worked through earlier chapters and can therefore
understand basic AutoCAD construction techniques.

When using a graphics tablet, commands are selected (picked)
from the overlay. The sequences describing how to construct the
Work Examples in this chapter have been considerably shortened
and will, in general, follow the pattern:

Overlay menu area	*Pick from overlay menu area*	*Command line prompts and required action*
1. **DRAW**	**LINE**	**From point:** 100,250
		To point: @0,150

The **DRAW** menu area of the overlay is shown in Fig. 5.5.

Work Example 5/1

1. **Main Menu**   **1. Begin a NEW drawing**
   Enter selection: 1
   Enter NAME of drawing: a:\ex05_01

When the AutoCAD drawing editor appears set LIMITS to 594,
420 (A2).

Overlay menu area	*Pick from overlay menu area*	*Command line prompts and required action*
2. **DRAW**	**LINE**	**From point:** 105,305
		To point: @60,0
		To point: @0,−150
		To point: @−60,0
		To point: c (close) to complete left-hand side of the development

3. Complete the outlines of the front, other side, top, bottom, tab
   and flaps as shown in Fig. 5.7, to the dimensions in Fig. 5.6

4. **EDIT**	**FILLET**	**Radius:** 5
		pick lines in turn to obtain fillets as in Fig. 5.7
5. **TEXT**	**STYLE**	romanc
		Height: 20
		Width factor <1>: *Ret*
		Obliquing angle <0>: *Ret*
		Backwards? <N>: *Ret*
		Upside-down? <N>: *Ret*
		Vertical <N>: *Ret*
6. **TEXT**	**TEXT**	Toggle to DTEXT
		Add text 50

7. Set styles and add text to drawings as in Figs 5.6 and 5.7

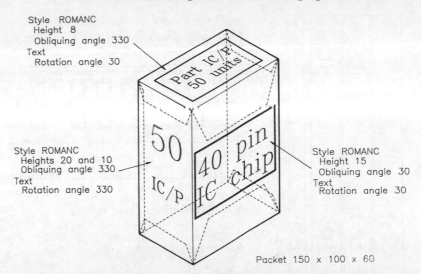

Style ROMANC
  Height 8
  Obliquing angle 330
Text
  Rotation angle 30

Style ROMANC
  Heights 20 and 10
  Obliquing angle 330
Text
  Rotation angle 330

Style ROMANC
  Height 15
  Obliquing angle 30
Text
  Rotation angle 30

Packet 150 x 100 x 60

Fig. 5.6 Isometric drawing
for Work Example 5/1

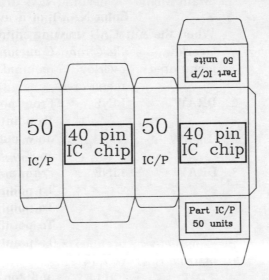

Fig. 5.7 Work Example 5/1

8.	**DRAW**	**PLINE**	Add plines of width 1
9.	**DRAW**	**LINE**	Add borders etc
10.	**TEXT**	**STYLE**	Set romans of height 8
11.	**TEXT**	**TEXT**	Add title An AutoCAD Workbook and Work Example 5/1
12.	**UTIL**	**SAVE**	ex05_01 Key

Work Example 5/2

1. **Main Menu**   1. Begin a NEW drawing
      Enter selection: 1

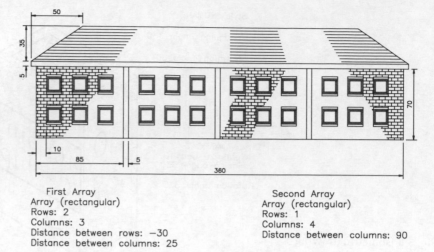

First Array
Array (rectangular)
Rows: 2
Columns: 3
Distance between rows: −30
Distance between columns: 25

Second Array
Array (rectangular)
Rows: 1
Columns: 4
Distance between columns: 90

Fig. 5.8 Work Example 5/2

Enter NAME of drawing: a:\ex05_02

When the AutoCAD drawing editor appears:

Overlay menu area	Pick from overlay menu area	Command line prompts and required action
2. **DRAW**	**LINE**	**From point:** 30, 215 *Key*
		To point: @360,0 *Key* continue to draw outlines of the front view of an 8-unit workshop given in Fig. 5.8
3. **DRAW**	**LINE**	**From point:** 40,205
		To point: @15,0
		To point: @0,−15
		To point: @−15,0
		To point: c (close)
4. **EDIT**	**OFFSET**	1
		pick top line
		continue *picking* to draw part of Fig. 5.9
5. **EDIT**	**OFFSET**	2
		pick top line
		pick bottom line to complete Fig. 5.9

Note: The **EDIT** menu area of the overlay is shown in Fig. 5.10.

6. **BLOCKS**	**WBLOCK**	**Block name (or ?):** window
		Block name: *Ret*
		Insertion base point: 40,190
		Select objects: w (window)

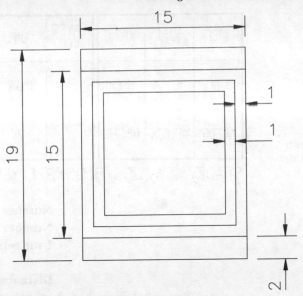

Fig. 5.9 Drawing of window
for Work Example 5/2

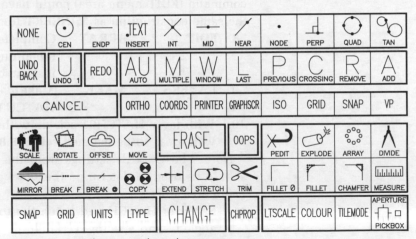

Fig. 5.10 The EDIT menu
area of the graphics tablet
overlay

OBJECT SNAP/TOGGLES/EDIT/SETTINGS

First corner: *pick* **Other corner:**
pick
30 found. Select objects: *Ret*
Note: The **BLOCKS** menu area of the overlay is shown in Fig.
5.11.
7. **BLOCKS**   **MINSERT** **Block name (or ?):** w (window)
Insertion point: 40,190
X scale factor: *Ret*
Y scale factor: *Ret*
Rotation angle <0>: *Ret*

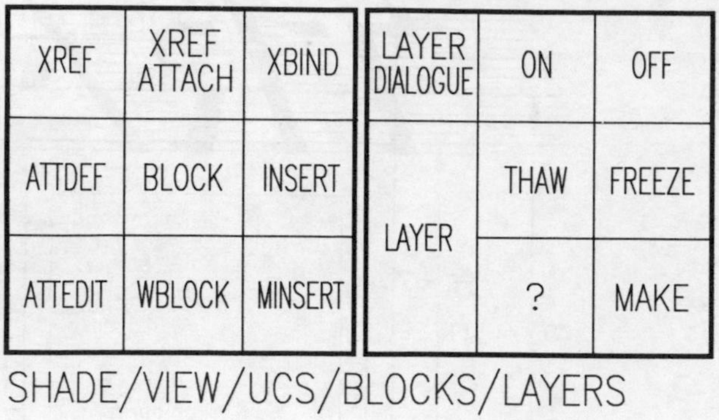

XREF	XREF ATTACH	XBIND
ATTDEF	BLOCK	INSERT
ATTEDIT	WBLOCK	MINSERT

LAYER DIALOGUE	ON	OFF
LAYER	THAW	FREEZE
	?	MAKE

SHADE/VIEW/UCS/BLOCKS/LAYERS

Fig. 5.11 The BLOCKS/LAYERS menu area of the graphics tablet overlay

Number of rows (——) <1>: 2
Number of columns (|||) <1>: 3
Unit cell or distance between rows: −30
Distance between columns: 25

Note: Figure 5.8 describes another method by which the **ARRAY** command (**EDIT** menu area) could have been employed to perform the same construction as **MINSERT** from the tablet overlay.

8. **EDIT**   **ARRAY**   Complete the addition of the remaining windows following the instructions in Fig. 5.8

9. **LAYERS**   **MAKE**   Make 2 layers HATCH and HATCH01 – colours red and yellow

10.   With layer HATCH01 set, draw the outlines of the roof and wall areas to be hatched – Fig. 5.8.

Note: The OSNAP settings from the menu area OBJECT SNAP should be used to determine the exact positions of the ends of the hatch area lines.

11.   Set layer HATCH and hatch the roof areas with style U at angle 0° and spacing 3. Hatch the wall areas with hatch style BRICK and scale 0.5.

Note: The command **HATCH** is not on the overlay.

12. **LAYERS**   **OFF**   Turn layer HATCH01 off
13. **UTIL**   **SAVE**   ex05_02

Work Example 5/3

1. **Main Menu**   **1. Begin a NEW drawing**
                       Enter selection: 1
                       Enter NAME of drawing: a:\ex05_03

When the AutoCAD drawing editor appears:

Layers: 0 — hatch shaded areas
colour white
hatching 0.3 spacing

outline — letter outlines
turned OFF
colour cyan

hatch — hatching 4 spacing
colour red

hatch01 — hatching outlines
turned OFF
colour yellow

Fig. 5.12 Work Example 5/3

Stage 1
Letter outlines
on Layer outline

Stage 2
Hatching on Layer 0

Stage 3
Hatch outlines on
Layer hatch01
Then Layers outline
and 0 turned OFF

Stage 4
Hatching on Layer
hatch
Then Layer hatch01
turned OFF
Then Layer 0
turned ON

Fig. 5.13 Stages in
constructing Work Example
5/3

Overlay menu area	Pick from overlay menu area	Command line prompts and required action
2. **DRAW**	**LINE**	Draw outline of the word TRAIN (Fig. 5.12)

3. Follow the sequences in Figs 5.12 and 5.13:
   Menu area **LAYERS** to make, to turn on and to turn off layers;
   Menu area **DRAW**, command **LINE** to draw outlines and lines
4. Add the WATER drawing of Fig. 5.14 below the TRAIN drawing:
   Menu area **DRAW**, command **PLINE** to draw both the word WATER (plines 2 wide, and the wave lines (plines 0 wide);
   Menu area **EDIT**, command **OFFSET** (set to 5 and 10) to copy wave lines

Fig. 5.14 The lower half of
Work Example 5/3

5. **UTIL**   **SAVE**   ex05_03 *Key*

Work Example 5/4

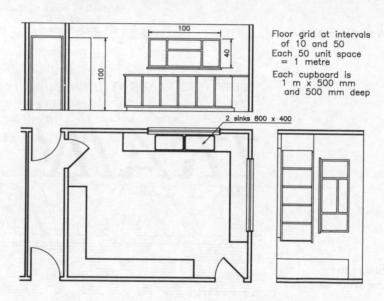

Floor grid at intervals
of 10 and 50
Each 50 unit space
= 1 metre

Each cupboard is
1 m x 500 mm
and 500 mm deep

2 sinks 800 x 400

Fig. 5.15 Work Example 5/4

Stage 1

1. **Main Menu**   **1. Begin a NEW drawing**
                    Enter selection: 1
                    Enter NAME of drawing: a:\ex05_04

When the AutoCAD drawing editor appears, set LIMITS to
594, 420 (A2).

Overlay menu area	Pick from overlay menu area	Command line prompts and required action
2. **LAYERS**	**MAKE**	Make a layer GRIDLINES colour yellow
3. **DRAW**	**LINE**	**From point:** 130,250
		To point: @250,0
		To point: *Ret*
		From point: 130,250
		To point: 0,−200

Start (130,250)

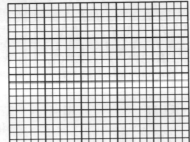

Fig. 5.16 Gridlines on which
Work Example 5/4 is started

			To point: *Ret*
4.	**EDIT**	**ARRAY**	Select vertical line and make a rectangular array of 26 columns at spacing of 10
5.	**EDIT**	**ARRAY**	Select horizontal line and make a rectangular array of 21 columns at spacing of −10
6.			**PEDIT** Key (**PEDIT** not on overlay)
7.			Change the original vertical and horizontal lines to plines 0.6 wide
8.	**EDIT**	**ARRAY**	Select vertical pline and make a rectangular array of 6 columns at spacing of 50
9.	**EDIT**	**ARRAY**	Select horizontal pline and make a rectangular array of 5 columns at spacing of −50
10.	**LAYERS**		Set layer 0
11.	**DRAW**	**PLINE**	With the grid as a guide draw the inner plines of the walls and partitions – plines of 1 unit width
12.	**EDIT**	**OFFSET**	Offset wall plines 5 units
13.	**EDIT**	**TRIM**	Trim plines as necessary
14.	**UTILS**	**SAVE**	ex05_04 (precautionary save)

Stage 2

1.	**DRAW**	**LINE**	Draw one line of each window in plan
2.	**EDIT**	**OFFSET**	Offset window lines by 2 and 3 unit
3.	**DRAW**	**LINE**	Draw outlines of windows in front and side views
4.	**EDIT**	**OFFSET**	Offset lines of windows by 2 in front and side views

5.	**DRAW**	**PLINE**	Set pline width to 1
			Add end lines of windows
			Add door lines
			Add outlines of cupboards in plan
6.	**DRAW**	**ARC**	Add arcs of doors
7.	**DRAW**	**LINE**	Add lines of cupboards in front and side views
8.	**EDIT**	**TRIM**	Trim lines in plan, front and side views as necessary
9.	Add text and lines to complete borders and titles		
10.	**UTILS**	**SAVE**	ex05_04

Introduction to Work Example 5/5

This Example is included here to give practice in the dimensioning. Only very limited descriptions of constructing the outlines of the three views and the adding of text and borders are given.

The drawing is constructed with LIMITS set to 594, 420 (A2).

Work Example 5/5

Stage 1

| 1. | **Main Menu** | **1. Begin a NEW drawing** |
| | | **Enter selection:** 1 |

THIRD ANGLE PROJECTION
Dimensions in millimetres

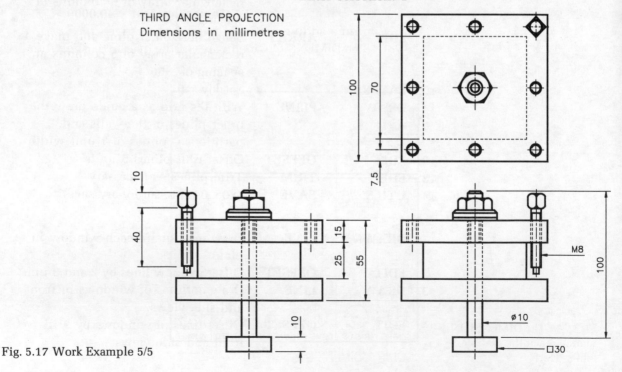

Fig. 5.17 Work Example 5/5

Enter NAME of drawing: a:\ex05_05

When the AutoCAD drawing editor appears:

Overlay menu area	*Pick from overlay menu area*	*Command line prompts and required action*
2. **LAYERS**	**MAKE**	Make layers:
		HIDDEN, yellow, hidden lines
		CENTRE, green, centre lines
		TEXT, cyan
		DIMNESN, blue
3.		Set layer 0
4. **DRAW**	**PLINE**	Draw the outlines of the views in plines of 0.7 unit width

5. Set layer HIDDEN and draw hidden detail (**DRAW – LINE**)
6. Set layer CENTRE and add centre lines (**DRAW – LINE**)
7. Set layer TEXT and add text – ROMANS style heights 6 and 8
8. **UTIL**   **SAVE**   ex05_05 (precautionary save)

Stage 2

1. Set layer DIMENSN
2. **DIMENSION VERT**   **First extension line origin:** *pick*
                                           Second extension line origin: *pick*
                                           Dimension line location: *pick*
                                           Dimension text <40.0000>: 40

3. Continue adding vertical dimensions as given in Fig. 5.17

Note: The DIMENSION menu area of the overlay is shown in Fig. 5.18.

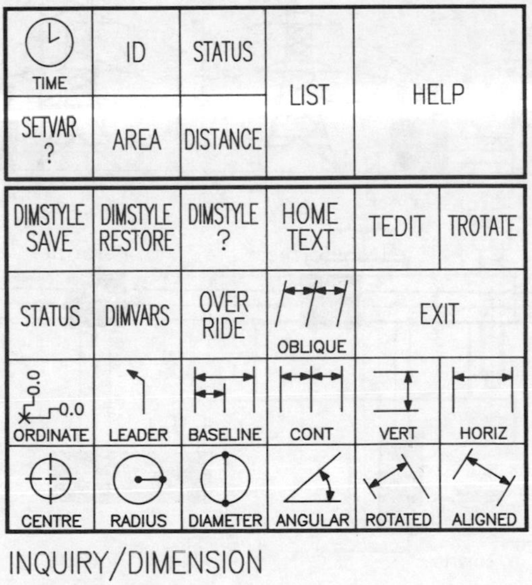

Fig. 5.18 The DIMENSION menu area of the graphics tablet overlay

4. **DIMENSION LEADER**   **Leader start:** *pick*
                          To point: *pick*
                          To point: *Ret*
                          Dimension text: %%c10

Note: %%c produces the diameter symbol prefixing the number 10

5.   Continue adding dimensions as given in Fig. 5.17
6. **UTILS**   **SAVE**   ex05_05

Introduction to Work Example 5/6

This Example is included here to show how a diagrammatic illustration can be constructed in AutoCAD. The drawing file for this Example is large containing some 300,000 bytes. Thus it may be necessary to ensure that the disk being used contains sufficient space to hold the file.

No new commands are used for this Example, so only the barest outline of each procedure necessary to construct the drawing is given. To assist the reader in following the sequence of drawing, four figures are given – Figs 5.19, 5.20, 5.21 and 5.22.

The positions of the various parts of the Example can be selected at the operator's discretion. This is not a drawing requiring precise dimensions. It is for illustrating how electric power is distributed from a power station to the places where power is required.

Work Example 5/6

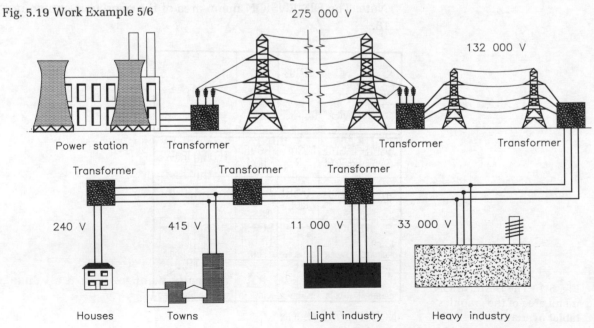

Fig. 5.19 Work Example 5/6

Stage 1

1. **Main Menu**   **1. Begin a NEW drawing**
    Enter selection: 1
    Enter NAME of drawing: a:\ex05_06
    When the AutoCAD drawing editor appears:
2. Set **LIMITS** to 297,210 (A4 sheet sizes). **LIMITS** is not on the
    overlay

Overlay menu area	Pick from overlay menu area	Command line prompts and required action
3. **DRAW**	**PLINE**	Draw the pline outline Fig. 5.19

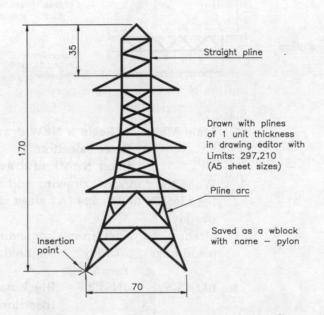

35

170

Straight pline

Drawn with plines
of 1 unit thickness
in drawing editor with
Limits: 297,210
(A5 sheet sizes)

Pline arc

Saved as a wblock
with name — pylon

Insertion point

70

Fig. 5.20 Drawing of pylon
WBLOCK for Work Example
5/6

4. **DRAW**	**LINE**	Draw the outlines of the cooling tower and transformer diagrams of Fig. 5.21
5. **DRAW**	**LINE**	With pline of width 1 unit, draw the base of the cooling tower and the insulator (Fig. 5.21)
6. Hatch the cooling tower and transformer drawings as shown in Fig. 5.21		
7. **BLOCKS**	**BLOCK**	Save each of the drawings as wblocks with filenames as in Figs 5.19 and 5.21
8. **UTIL**	**QUIT**	**Really want to discard all changes to drawing:** y (yes)

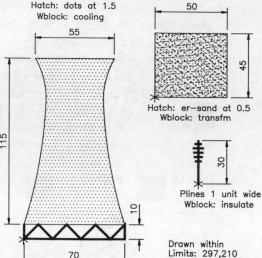

Hatch: dots at 1.5
Wblock: cooling

55

115

70

10

50

45

Hatch: er—sand at 0.5
Wblock: transfm

30

Plines 1 unit wide
Wblock: insulate

Drawn within
Limits: 297,210
✳ Insertion points

Fig. 5.21 Drawings of other
WBLOCKs for Work
Example 5/6

Stage 2

1. **Main Menu   1. Begin a NEW drawing**
   Enter selection: 1
   Enter NAME of drawing: a:\ex05_06

   When the AutoCAD drawing editor appears:

2. Set **LIMITS** to 840,594 (A1 sheet sizes). **LIMITS** is not on the overlay

Overlay menu area	Pick from overlay menu area	Command line prompts and required action

3. **BLOCKS   INSERT   Block name:** pylon
   Insertion point: pick
   X scale factor: 0.8 Key
   Y scale factor: Ret
   Rotation angle <0>: Ret

4. Continue inserting wblocks pylon, cooling, transfm and insulate as indicated by Fig. 5.22

5. **UTILS   SAVE   ex05_06** (precautionary save)

6. Working to suitable sizes add further details as given in Fig. 5.19

7. Hatch parts of the construction just drawn with suitable hatch patterns from the dialogue box **Select Hatch Pattern** from the **Options** *pull-down* menu

8. **UTILS   SAVE   ex05_06**

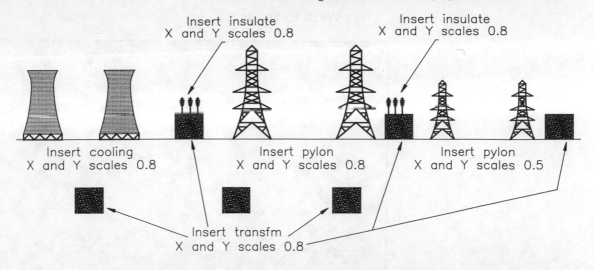

Insert insulate
X and Y scales 0.8

Insert insulate
X and Y scales 0.8

Insert cooling
X and Y scales 0.8

Insert pylon
X and Y scales 0.8

Insert pylon
X and Y scales 0.5

Insert transfm
X and Y scales 0.8

Drawing constructed within limits 840 × 594 (A1)

Fig. 5.22 Insert positions of
WBLOCKs for Work
Example 5/6

Work Example 5/7

Car parking booking	
To be completed by driver and left at the booking office.	
Name of driver	
Car registration	
Time of arrival	
Time of departure	
Method of payment and charge To be completed by attendant at end of parking period.	
Cash Yes ☐ No ☐ Cheque Yes ☐ No ☐ Credit card Yes ☐ No ☐	
Credit card number	
Charge per hour	
COST	

Fig. 5.23 Work Example 5/7

No instructions are given for this Example. The styles for the text are:

> ROMANC – height 10
> ROMANC – height 6
> ROMAND – height 6
> ROMANS – heights 5 and 6

The outlines are lines or plines (1 unit wide).

Work Example 5/8

Fig. 5.24 Work Example 5/8

1. **Main Menu   1. Begin a NEW drawing**
    Enter selection: 1
    Enter NAME of drawing: a:\ex05_08
    When the AutoCAD drawing editor appears:

Overlay menu area	*Pick from overlay menu area*	*Command line prompts and required action*

2. **DRAW   LINE   From point:** any
                                To point: @20,−30
                                To point: *Ret*

3. **EDIT   OFFSET**   Offset 2 lines at distance 2.5

4. Repeat with **LINE** and **PLINE** (1 unit wide), followed by **TRIM** to obtain shape as in Fig. 5.25

5. Follow the stages given in Fig. 5.25. The **ROTATE** prompts and responses follow the pattern:

    EDIT   ROTATE   Select objects: w (window)
                                First corner: *pick* **Other corner:** *pick*
                                window original shape **12 found**
                                Select objects: *Ret*
                                Base point: *pick*
                                Rotation angle: 90
                                Command:

    Note: This rotates the original shape to lie horizontally.

6. **EDIT   ARRAY   Select objects:** w (window)

Stage 1 Stage 2 Stage 3

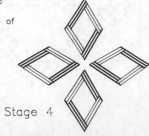

Copy and Rotate
through 90°

Move shapes to positions

Plines are 0.6 wide
Plines are offset 2.5
Lines are offset 2.5
Trim unwanted parts of
plines and lines

Stage 4

Mirror — first vertical shape
then horizontal shape

Fig. 5.25 Stages in
constructions for Work
Example 5/8

window the horizontal shapes
Select objects: *Ret*
Rectangular or Polar array?: r
(rectangular)
Number of rows: 3
Number of columns: 6
Distance between rows: −135
Distance between columns: 67.5

Repeat with the 2 vertical shapes — 4 rows at −67.5; 3 columns at 135

7. Add borders and text to complete the construction

8. **EDIT** **TRIM** Trim parts of the pattern which
appear beyond all the drawing
border lines

9. **UTIL** **SAVE** ex05_08

Work Example 5/9

1. **Main Menu** **1. Begin a NEW drawing**
Enter selection: 1
Enter NAME of drawing: a:\ex05_09
When the AutoCAD drawing editor appears:
Overlay *Pick from* *Command line prompts and*
menu area *overlay* *required action*
menu area

2. **DRAW** **PLINE** **From point:** pick any point
Width: 6
To point: @6,0

Fig. 5.26 Work Example 5/9

		To point: *Ret*	
	Note: This forms a square of sides 6 units long.		
3.	**EDIT**	**COPY**	Copy the 6 unit square 4 times to obtain 5 identical squares anywhere on the screen
4.	**EDIT**	**CHANGE**	Change the colours of the squares to obtain squares of colour green, red, blue, yellow, white
5.	**EDIT**	**COPY**	With multiple **COPY**, copy each colour square in turn, with its **Base point of displacement:** at the centre of the square. With **Snap** set to 10 copy the squares to form the pattern in Fig. 5.26
6.	**UTIL**	**SAVE**	ex05_09

Work Example 5/10

1.	**Main Menu**	**1. Begin a NEW drawing**
		Enter selection: 1
		Enter NAME of drawing: a:\ex05_10

The reader should be able to construct this Example from the information given in Fig. 5.28 and use judgement on sizes and positions of the various parts of the drawing as shown in Fig. 5.27.

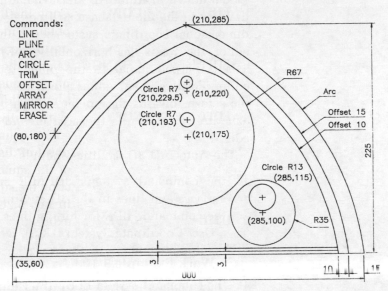

Commands:
LINE
PLINE
ARC
CIRCLE
TRIM
OFFSET
ARRAY
MIRROR
ERASE

Fig. 5.28 First stage of the construction for Work Example 5/10

CHAPTER 6

3D drawing

Introduction

The 3D facilities of AutoCAD allow the operator to construct drawings of models in three-dimensional space. When a file of a 3D model drawn in AutoCAD are saved, all 3D data are saved with the drawing in the file database. 3D models are constructed in a three-dimensional coordinate system x,y,z. In the plane of the drawing editor, the x axis lies horizontally and the y axis vertically. The z axis is perpendicular to the plane represented by the drawing editor. Positive (+ve) values along the z axis are as if coming out of the screen towards the operator; negative (-ve) values along the z axis are as if towards the area behind the plane of the drawing editor.

The AutoCAD 3D facilities include:

1. the command systems 3DFACE and LINE for constructing surfaces and lines in the 3D environment;
2. the command HIDE for hiding lines lying behind 3d faces;
3. a User Coordinate System (UCS), which allows the operator to manipulate planes in the x,y,z space on which to construct models;
4. the command system ELEV (Elevation) for extruding objects in the direction of the z axis;
5. a number of 3D objects held in the file *3d.lsp*;
6. a number of surface commands – EDGSURF, REVSURF, RULSURF and TABSURF – for the construction of flat or approximately curved surfaces;
7. the VPOINT and DVIEW (dynamic view) command systems for viewing 3D models from a variety of positions;
8. the Advanced Modelling Extension (AME) for constructing solid models is available for AutoCAD Release 11.

Work Examples based on the AME system will be found in the next two chapters of this book.

Notes

1. Solid models can only be constructed in MSPACE.
2. TILEMODE can be either ON (1) or OFF (0) when constructing 3D models. If, however, 3D models or pictorial views from 3D models (e.g. with VPOINT or DVIEW) are to be included with title blocks or orthographic views, the following procedure must be adopted:

   Command: TILEMODE<1>: 0 (OFF) – sets up PSPACE
   Command: LIMITS: check if screen limits have changed
   Command: MVIEW: state the number of viewports required
   Command: MSPACE: to allow 3D models to be constructed
   Command: PSPACE to construct orthographic views

3. The full set of Advanced Modelling Extension facilities for solid drawing are only available with the optional package AME. However a limited number of the facilities from the AME package are available with the standard AutoCAD Release 11.
4. If working in the User Coordinate System (UCS), the variable UCSFOLLOW must be set to 1 (ON). If the variable is not set to on the UCS planes will not change when required to do so, but will stay in the WORLD UCS plane. The variable is set as follows:

   Command: UCSFOLLOW<0>: 1

5. Commands can be typed at the keyboard, selected from pull-down or on-screen menus, or selected from a graphics tablet. The menu area of the AutoCAD Release 11 overlay with some of the commands included in this chapter is shown in Fig. 6.19 on page 139.
6. When constructing 3D models, and typing commands at the keyboard, the following abbreviations are available if standard AutoCAD software is in use:

   DV – DVIEW (Chapter 9);
   MS – MSPACE (Chapter 8);
   PS – PSPACE (Chapter 8);
   VP – VPOINT;
   H – HIDE.

Introduction to Work Example 6/1

In this Work Example, four simple 3D models are constructed with the aid of the commands:

3DFACE – to form the surfaces of the models;
VPOINT – to place the 3D models in a viewing position on screen as if seen from the front right and from above;
HIDE – to remove hidden lines from the models on screen.

Note: 3DFACEs in AutoCAD are basically triangles or quadrilaterals. If a 3DFACE with more than four edges is to be constructed, it must be made up from adjoining quadrilaterals. This means that adjoining edges of the quadrilaterals (and/or triangles) making up a complex face may need to be made invisible. If not made invisible, 3D models in AutoCAD will show as wireframes consisting of a series of adjacent 3DFACEs. An example of the use of the **invisible** facility of the **3DFACE** command is given in the 3D model 4 of Work Example 6/1 (Figure 6.1).

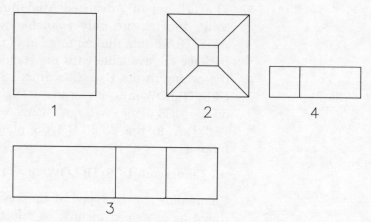

Fig. 6.1 Work Example 6/1

When constructing the 3D model 1 of Fig. 6.1, each corner of each 3DFACE is determined by keying in its x,y,z coordinate numbers from the keyboard.

When constructing the 3D models 2 and 3 of Fig. 6.1, the x,y,z coordinates are determined by first selecting .XY from the FILTERS pull-down menu, or from the 3DFACE on-screen menu; then keying in the x,y coordinate numbers (or picking the x,y position on screen with the aid of the selection device); then keying in the required z coordinate number when prompted to do so. The procedure follows the pattern:

Command or Prompt –   *Key, select from Filters or from*
key, select from pull-   *3dface on-screen menu*
downs, or from on-screen
menus

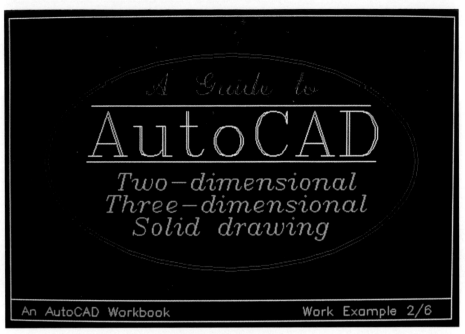

Plate I   The screen view of Work Example 2/6

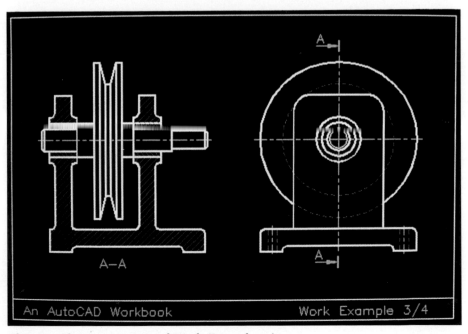

Plate II   The screen view of Work Example 3/4

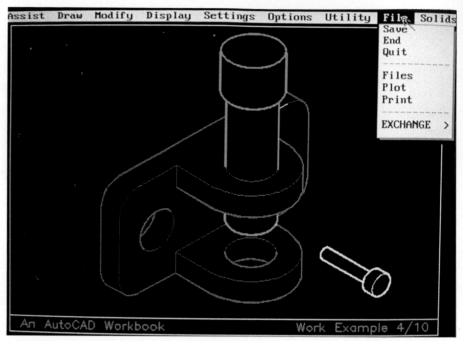

Plate III   The screen view of Work Example 4/10 with File pull-down menu

Plate IV   The screen view of Work Example 5/4

Plate V The screen view of Work Example 5/3

Plate VI A colour plot of Work Example 5/3

Plate VII   The screen view of Work Example 5/10

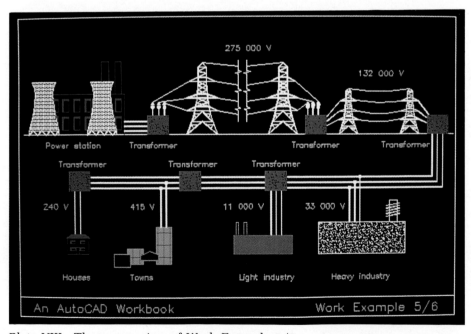

Plate VIII   The screen view of Work Example 5/6

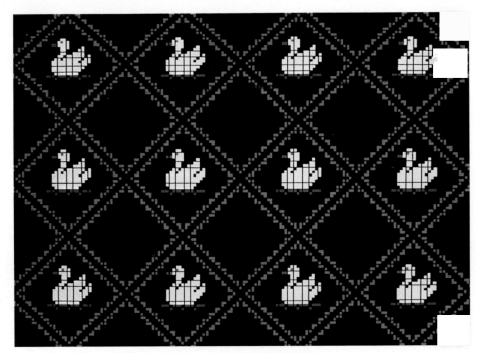

Plate IX   The screen view of an embroidery design

Plate X   A colour plot of the embroidery design

Plate XI A second embroidery design with the Assist pull-down menu

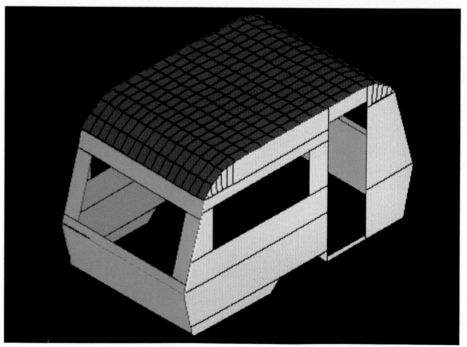

Plate XII A SHADE view of a 3D model drawing of a caravan shell

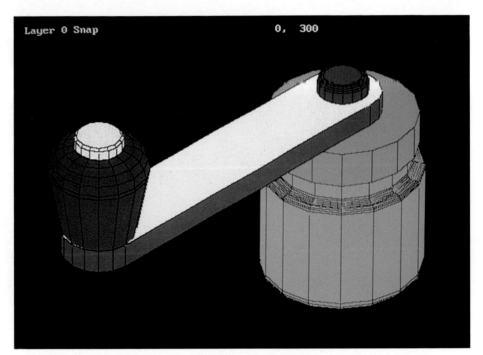

Plate XIII   A SHADE view of a 3D solid model drawing

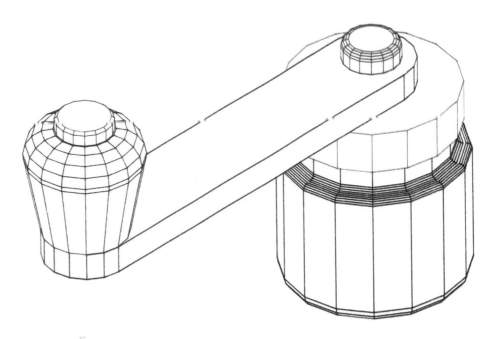

Plate XIV   A colour plot of the 3D solid model shown in Plate XIII

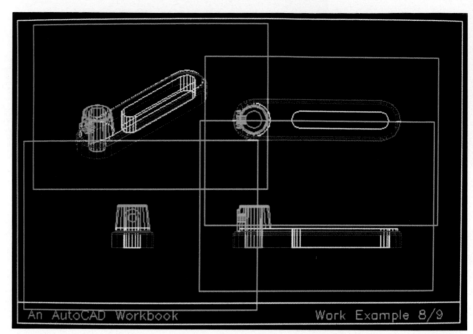

An AutoCAD Workbook

Work Example 8/9

Plate XV A 3D AME solid model drawing in four viewports, with the viewports moved to obtain a good orthographic projection

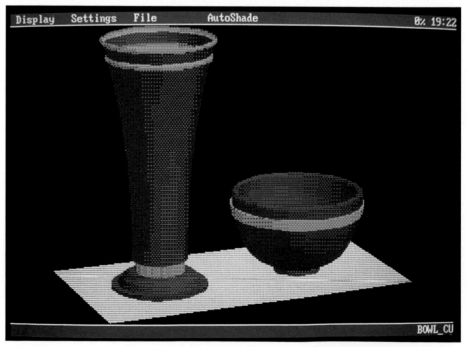

Display   Settings   File   AutoShade   0% 19:22

BOWL_CU

Plate XVI   An AutoShade view of two AME 2 3D solid model drawings

Command: 3DFACE
First point: .xy
.xy of   numbers or *pick* on screen
(need Z):   z number
Second point:

see Fig. 6.2.

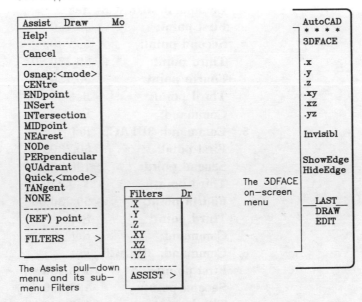

Fig. 6.2 The Filters
pull-down and 3DFACE on
screen menus

Work Example 6/1

1.   **Main Menu   1. Begin a NEW drawing**
                   Enter name of drawing ex06_01

3D model 1 (Fig. 6/1)

Command or Prompt	Key, select from	Result
— key, select from	Filters or from 3dface	
pull-downs, or from	on-screen menu	
on-screen menus		

2.   **Command: 3DFACE**   Ret
     First point: 50,150
     Second point: 130,150
     Third point: 130,230
     Fourth point: 50,230
     Third point: *Ret*
     Command: *Ret*   Base of cube
                                         drawn

3.   **Command: 3DFACE**   Ret
     First point: 50,150

Second point:	130,150	
Third point:	130,150,80	
Fourth point:	50,150,80	
Third point:	*Ret*	
Command:	*Ret*	Front face drawn

4. **Command: 3DFACE** *Ret*

First point:	50,150	
Second point:	50,230,	
Third point:	50,230,80	
Fourth point:	50,150,80	
Third point:	*Ret*	
Command:	*Ret*	Left face drawn

5. **Command: 3DFACE** *Ret*

First point:	50,230	
Second point:	130,230	
Third point:	130,230,80	
Fourth point:	50,230,80	
Third point:	*Ret*	
Command:	*Ret*	Back face drawn

6. **Command: 3DFACE** *Ret*

First point:	130,150	
Second point:	130,230	
Third point:	130,230,80	
Fourth point:	130,150,80	
Third point:	*Ret*	
Command:	*Ret*	Right face drawn

7. **Command: 3DFACE** *Ret*

First point:	50,150,80	
Second point:	50,230,80	
Third point:	130,230,80	
Fourth point:	130,150,80	
Third point:	*Ret*	
Command:	*Ret*	Top drawn

8. **Command: VPOINT** −1,−1,1

The drawing is displayed on screen in pictorial form. Lines behind 3DFACEs removed

9. **Command: HIDE**

10. **Command: SAVE**   – precautionary SAVE

to avoid possible loss
of drawing

3D model 2 (Fig. 6.1)

Command or Prompt – key, select from pull-downs, or from on-screen menus	Key, select from Filters or from 3dface on-screen menu	Result
1. **Command: 3DFACE:**		
First point:	200,150	
Second point:	280,150	
Third point:	280,230	
Fourth point:	200,230	
Third point:	Ret	
Command:	Ret	Base drawn
2. **Command: 3DFACE:**		
First point:	.xy	
.xy of	230,200	
(need Z):	100	
Second point:	.xy	
.xy of	250,200	
(need Z):	100	
Third point:	.xy	
.xy of	250,180	
(need Z):	100	
Fourth point:	.xy	
.xy of	230,180	
(need Z):	100	
Third point:	Ret	
Command:	Ret	Top face drawn
3. **Command: 3DFACE:**		
First point:	200,150	
Second point:	200,230	
Third point:	.xy	
.xy of	230,200	
(need Z):	100	
Fourth point:	.xy	
.xy of	230,180	
(need Z):	100	
Third point:	Ret	
Command:	Ret	Left face drawn
4. **Command: 3DFACE:**		
First point:	280,150	
Second point:	280,230	

Third point:	.xy	
.xy of	250,200	
(need Z):	100	
Fourth point:	.xy	
.xy of	250,180	
(need Z):	100	
Third point:	*Ret*	
Command:	*Ret*	Right face drawn

5. **Command: 3DFACE:**

First point:	200,150	
Second point:	280,150	
Third point:	.xy	
.xy of	250,180	
(need Z):	100	
Fourth point:	.xy	
.xy of	230,180	
(need Z):	100	
Third point:	*Ret*	
Command:	*Ret*	Front face drawn

6. **Command: 3DFACE:**

First point:	200,230	
Second point:	280,230	
Third point:	.xy	
.xy of	250,200	
(need Z):	100	
Fourth point:	.xy	
.xy of	230,200	
(need Z):	100	
Third point:	*Ret*	
Command:	*Ret*	Back face drawn

7. **Command: VPOINT** −1,−1,1   Drawing on screen in pictorial form

8. **Command: HIDE**   Lines behind 3DFACEs removed

9. **Command: SAVE**   − precautionary SAVE to avoid possible loss of drawing

3D model 3 (Fig. 6.1)

Command or Prompt Key, select from
− key, select from   Filters or from 3dface

pull-downs or from   on-screen menus
on-screen menus

1. **Command: 3DFACE:**
   First point: 50,50
   Second point: 250,50
   Third point: 250,100
   Fourth point: 50,100
   Third point: *Ret*
   Command: *Ret*   Base drawn

2. **Command: 3DFACE:**
   First point: 50,50
   Second point: 50,100
   .xy of   150,100
   (need Z):   50
   Third point: .xy
   .xy of   150,50
   (need Z):   50
   Fourth point: .xy pick
   .xy of   150,50
   (need Z):   50
   Third point: *Ret*
   Command: *Ret*   Slope face
                                           drawn

3. **Command: 3DFACE:**
   First point: .xy
   .xy of   150,50
   (need Z):   50
   Second point: .xy
   .xy of   150,100
   (need Z):   50
   Third point: .xy
   .xy of   250,100
   (need Z):   50
   Fourth point: .xy
   .xy of   250,50
   (need Z):   50
   Third point: *Ret*
   Command: *Ret*   Top face drawn

4. **Command: 3DFACE:**
   First point: .xy
   .xy of   250,50
   (need Z):   20
   Second point: .xy

.xy of	250,100	
(need Z):	20	
Third point:	.xy	
.xy of	200,100	
(need Z):	20	
Fourth point:	.xy	
.xy of	200,50	
(need Z):	20	
Third point:	*Ret*	
Command:	*Ret*	Slot base drawn

5. **Command: 3DFACE:**

First point:	.xy	
.xy of	250,50	
(need Z):	30	
Second point:	.xy	
.xy of	250,100	
(need Z):	30	
Third point:	.xy	
.xy of	200,100	
(need Z):	30	
Fourth point:	.xy	
.xy of	200,50	
(need Z):	30	
Third point:	*Ret*	
Command:	*Ret*	Top of slot drawn

6. **Command: 3DFACE:**

First point:	.xy	
.xy of	200,50	
(need Z):	20	
Second point:	.xy	
.xy of	200,50	
(need Z):	30	
Third point:	.xy	
.xy of	200,100	
(need Z):	30	
Fourth point:	.xy	
.xy of	200,100	
(need Z):	20	
Third point:	*Ret*	
Command:	*Ret*	Right end of slot

7. **Command: 3DFACE:**

First point:	250,50	

Second point:	250,100	
Third point:	.xy	
.xy of	250,100	
(need Z):	20	
Fourth point:	.xy	
.xy of	250,50	
(need Z):	20	
Third point:	Ret	
Command:	Ret	Lower right end drawn

Then the sequence as follows using the same methods:

8. Upper right end:
   250,50,30; 250,100,30; 250,100,50; 250,50,50
9. Front face:
   50,50; 200,50; 200,50,50; 150,50,50
10. Front below slot:
    200,50; 250,50; 250,50,20; 200,50,20
11. Front above slot:
    200,50,30; 200,50,50; 250,50,50; 250,50,30
12. Rear face:
    50,100; 200,100; 200,100,50; 150,100,50
13. Rear below slot:
    200,100; 250,100; 250,100,20; 200,100,20
14. Rear above slot:
    200,100,30; 200,100,50; 250,100,50; 250,100,30

15. **Command: VPOINT** $-1,-1,1$	The drawing is displayed on screen in pictorial form
16. **Command: HIDE**	Lines behind 3Dfaces removed
17. **Command: SAVE**	– precautionary SAVE to avoid possible loss of drawing

3D model 4 (Fig. 6.1)

Command or Prompt – key, select from pull-downs or from on-screen menus	Key, select from Filters or from 3dface on-screen menus	Result
1. **Command: 3DFACE:**		
First point:	i (invisible)	2 edges

	330,150	of 3dface
Second point:	i (invisible)	invisible
	.xy	
.xy of	330,150	
(need Z):	30	
Third point:	.xy	
.xy of	300,150	
(need Z):	30	
Fourth point:	300,150	
Third point:	Ret	
Command:	Ret	

Go on to complete the 3D model following the same routines as for Examples 2 and 3.

2. **Command:** SAVE ex06_01

At any time during the construction of each of the 3D models of Fig. 6.1, they can be viewed as if seen from above and from the right with the aid of the VPOINT command as follows:

Command/Prompt	Action	Result
Command: VPOINT	Key Ret	
<0.0000,0.0000,0.0000>	−1,−1,1 Key Ret	3D view of models appears on screen
Command: HIDE	Ret	Hidden lines removed

The result of VPOINT with x,y,z at −1,−1,1 of all four 3D models is shown in Fig. 6.3.

Note: To revert to a previous screen after VPOINT key u (for UNDO).

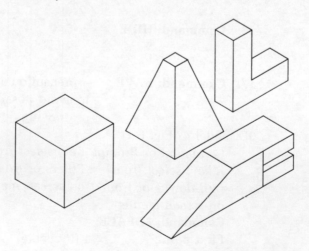

Fig. 6.3 VPOINT view of Work Example 6/1

Work Example 6/2

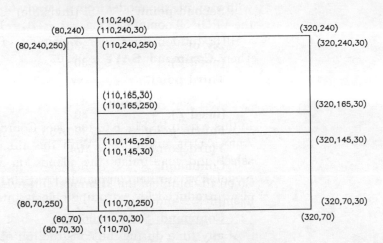

(80,240) (110,240)
(110,240,30)   (320,240)
(80,240,250)   (110,240,250)   (320,240,30)

(110,165,30)
(110,165,250)   (320,165,30)

(110,145,250)   (320,145,30)
(110,145,30)

(80,70,250)   (110,70,250)   (320,70,30)
(80,70)   (110,70,30)   (320,70)
(80,70,30)   (110,70)

Fig. 6.4 Work Example 6/2

1. **Main Menu   1. Begin a NEW drawing**
                  Enter name of drawing ex06_02

Figure 6.4 is the plan view of a 3D model of a simple angle bracket
which includes a supporting web. All the x,y,z coordinate points of
the corners of the 3DFACEs for constructing the model are given in
the drawing. A VPOINT view of the model (viewed from x,y,z
= −1,−1,1) is given in Fig. 6.5.

Using the methods given for constructing the four 3D models of

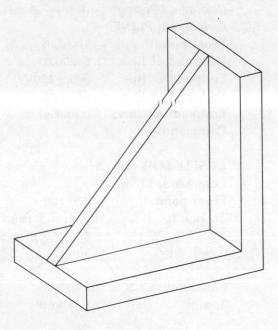

Fig. 6.5 VPOINT view of
Work Example 6/2

Fig. 6.1, construct a 3D model of the angle bracket and experiment with viewing the model from a variety of viewpoints with the aid of the VPOINT command: e.g. −1,−1,1; −1,1,1; 1,−1,1; 1,1,−1, etc.

HIDE hidden lines after each new VPOINT appears on screen. Then: **Command: SAVE** ex06_02

Work Example 6/3

In this example (Fig. 6.6) the User Coordinate System (the UCS) of AutoCAD is introduced. With the aid of the UCS, the user can select and manipulate the planes on which to construct a 3D model. Two further commands TABSURF and ELEV (Elevation) are also introduced for extruding objects into 3D space.

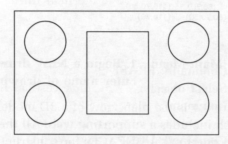

Fig. 6.6 Work Example 6/3

1. **Main Menu   1. Begin a NEW drawing**
    Enter name of drawing ex06_03
    When the AutoCAD drawing editor appears:

Command/Prompt	Action/Coords	Result
2. **Command: PLINE**		
From point:	100,220	
Endpoint of line:	@200,0	
Endpoint of line:	@0,−120	
Endpoint of line:	@−200,0	
Endpoint of line:	c (close)	
Command:		Pline rectangle drawn
3. **UCSFOLLOW<0>: 1**		
4. **Command: LINE**		
From point:	320,100	
To point:	.xy (*pick from Filters*)	
.xy of	320,100 *pick or Key*	
(need Z):	50	Vertical line 50 high
5. **Command: UCS**		
3point	3 (3point)	

Origin point:	100,100	
Point on X-axis:	350,100	
Point on X–Y plane:	.xy (*pick* from Filters)	
.xy of	350,100 *pick* Key	
(need Z):	100	UCS changes to front view of the plinc

6. **Surfaces. . .** from
   Draw *pull-down*

Tabulated surfaces	*pick*	
Select path curve:	*pick* the pline	
Select direction		
vector:	*pick* bottom end of the vertical line	Pline is extruded to height of 50 units

7. **Command: ERASE**

Select objects:	*pick* vertical line	
Command:		Vertical line erased

8. **Command: UCS**   w (World)   Plan view returns

9. **Command: 3DFACE**

First point:	100,100,50	
Second point:	@200,0,0	
Third point:	@0,120,0	
Fourth point:	@−200,0,0	
Third point:	*Ret Ret* (yes twice)	
Command:		3dface on extrusion

10. **Command: ELEV**

New elevation:	50	
New thickness:	25	Elevation set at 25
Command:		high, 50 above x,y plane

11. **Command: CIRCLE:**

Center point:	130,190	
Radius:	20	Cylinder 25 high, 50 above x,y plane

12. **Command: COPY**
    Select objects: *pick* circle
    Base point
    <Multiple>:   m (Multiple)
    Base point: *pick* circle centre
    Second point: *pick* each of other 3
                                circles positions in
                                turn *Ret*   All 4 cylinders
                                                               drawn
    Command:

13. **Command: LINE**
    From point: 170,120
    To point: @60,0
    To point: @0,80
    To point: @−60,0
    To point: c (close)   25 high block
                                                               drawn
    Command: 50 above x,y
                                                               plane

14. **Command: ELEV**
    New elevation: 0
    New thickness: 0   Elevation re-set
    Command: on x,y plane

15. **Command: 3DFACE**
    First point: 170,120,75
    Second point: @60,0,0
    Third point: @0,80,0
    Fourth point: @−60,0,0
    Third point: *Ret*   3dface on top
    Command: of rectangle

16. **Command: VPOINT**
    <0.0000,0.0000.
    1.0000>   −1,−1,1
    Regenerating
    drawing   New viewpoint
                                                               drawing

17. **Command: HIDE**   **Regenerating drawing**   Hidden lines
                                                       removed

18. **Command: SAVE**   ex06_03

Note: The VPOINT command can be called at any time during this construction to show the 3D model in a pictorial view.

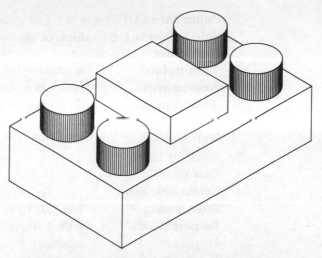

Fig. 6.7 VPOINT view of
Work Example 6/3

Introduction to Work Example 6/4

In the following sequences, the descriptions of each process are less detailed than in previous Work Examples.

Coordinate points can be either picked with a mouse, puck or stylus or typed at the keyboard. If typed at the keyboard each set of coordinates must be followed by pressing the Return key of the keyboard, mouse, puck or stylus. If the coordinate point requires a z coordinate this can be typed in or .XY can be selected from Filters from the 3DFACE on-screen sub-menu.

Work Example 6/4

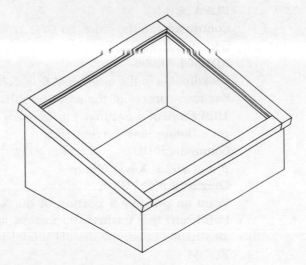

Fig. 6.8 Work Example 6/4

1. **Main Menu   1. Begin a NEW drawing**
   Enter name of drawing ex06_04
2. **3DFACE**

First point:	80,70
Second point:	@0,180
Third point:	@0,0,100
Fourth point:	80,70,60
Third point:	Ret

3. **UCSFOLLOW<0>:**   1
4. **COPY**

Select objects:	*pick* last drawn 3dface
Base point:	*pick* 80,70
Second point:	*pick* 380,70 (or *Key* @300,0)

Note: The 3DFACE has now been copied as a second side.

5. **VPOINT:** −1,−1,1 (to check the two faces)
6. **UNDO** (or u returns to the World UCS)
7. **3DFACE**

   coordinates in the order: 85,75; @0,170; @0,0,99; 85,75,61; four corners of the required 3dface
8. **COPY**

   Copy the last drawn 3dface from 85,75 to 295,75
9. **3DFACE**

   coordinates in the order: 80,250; @300,0; @0,0,100; @-300,0,0; the four corners of the required 3dface
10. **3DFACE**

    coordinates in the order: 80,70; 380,70; 380,70,60; 80,70,60; the four corners of the required 3dface
11. **3DFACE**

    coordinates in the order: 85,245; 375,245; 375,245,99; 85,245,99; the four corners of the required 3dface
12. **3DFACE**

    coordinates in the order: 85,75; 375,75; 375,75,61; 85,75,61; the four corners of the required 3dface
13. **UCS Control – Settings** *pull-down*

    pick **Define new current UCS**
    Name SIDE
    pick **Origin, Xaxis, Plane**
    Origin<0,0,0>: 80,70
    Point on positive-Y portion of the X-axis: 80,250
    Point on the positive-Y portion of the UCS X-Y plane: 80,70,100
14. **ZOOM** 1

15. **UCS Control – Settings** *pull-down*
     pick **Define new current UCS**
     Name TOPFRAME
     pick **Origin, Xaxis, Plane**
     Origin<0,0,0>: 0,60
     Point on positive-Y portion of the X-axis: 180,100
     Point on the positive-Y portion of the UCS X Y plano:
     0,60,100

     Note: The current **UCS** is now set so that it is lying on the tops of
     the sides of the coldframe box.

16. **ZOOM** 1

17. **Layer Control – Settings** *pull-down*
     Make a new layer TOPFRAME – colour yellow. Make it the
     current layer. Turn Layer 0 off.

18. **3DFACE**
     Make 3dfaces as follows – only coordinates of corners given:

     Face 1: −5,305; 190,305; 190,290; −5,290
     Face 2: −5,305; −5,305,−10; 190,305,−10; 190,305
     Face 3: −5,305,−10; −5,290,−10; 190,290,−10; 190,305,−10
     Face 4: −5,305; −5,290; −5,290,−10; −5,305,−10
     Face 5: −5,290; 190,290; 190,290,−10; −5,290,−10
     Face 6: 190,305; 190,290; 190,290,−10; 190,305,−10

19. **COPY**
     Copy the last drawn set of six faces in a copy window from
     −5,290 to −5,−5

20. **3DFACE**
     Make 3dfaces as follows – only coordinates of corners given:
     Face 1: −5,290; −5,10; 10,10; 10,290
     Face 2: −5,290; −5,10; −5,10,−10; −5,290,−10
     Face 3: −5,290,−10; −5,10,−10; 10,10,−10; 10,290,−10
     Face 4: 10,290; 10, 10,290, 10,10; 10,10, 10

21. **COPY**
     Copy the last group of 3dfaces in a copy window from 10,10 to
     190,10

22. **LINE**
     From point: 10,290,−4
     To point: 175,290,−4
     To point: 175,10,−4
     To point: 10,10,−4
     To point: c (close)

23. **LINE**
     As 21 above but with each z coordinate as −6

24. **VPOINT** −1,−1,1. Turn Layer0 on.

25. **HIDE**
26. **SAVE** ex06_04

Introduction to Work Example 6/5 (Fig. 6.10)

In this Work Example solids of revolution are constructed with the aid of REVSURF. This entails the drawing of the outline of the solids – path curves. It is best if path curves are continuous PLINEs. If made up of objects such as LINEs and/or ARCs, each line or arc must be acted upon to form the solid. The settings of the two variables SURFTAB1 and SURFTAB2 determine the mesh density of the solids.

Work Example 6/5

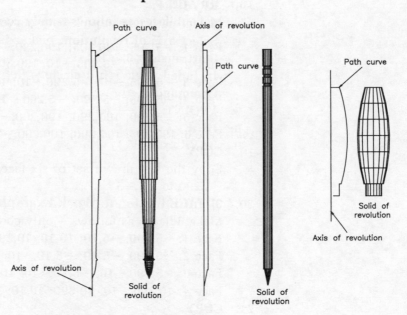

Fig. 6.9 First stage of Work Example 6/5

1. **Begin a NEW drawing**
   Enter name of drawing: ex06_05
2. **PLINE**

With the drawings of path curves of Fig. 6.9 as guides, construct suitable path curves

3. **LINE**

Draw the paths of revolution – they must be straight lines or plines

4. **SURFTAB1**
   New value for SURFTAB1 <6>: 16
5. **SURFTAB2 <6>:** Ret

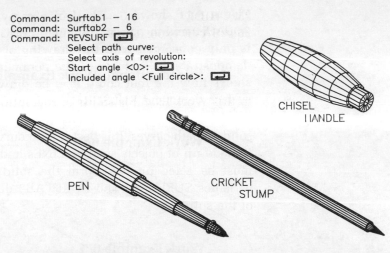

```
Command: Surftab1 - 16
Command: Surftab2 - 6
Command: REVSURF [⏎]
         Select path curve:
         Select axis of revolution:
         Start angle <0>: [⏎]
         Included angle <Full circle>: [⏎]
```

CHISEL
HANDLE

PEN

CRICKET
STUMP

Fig. 6.10 Work Example 6/5

6. **REVSURF:**
   Select path curve: *pick* path curve pline
   Select axis of revolution: *pick* axis of revolution
   Start angle <0>: *Ret*
   Included angle <full circle>: *Ret*
   Command:
7. **VPOINT:** −1,−1,1
8. **HIDE**
9. **SAVE** ex06_05

Introduction to Work Example 6/6

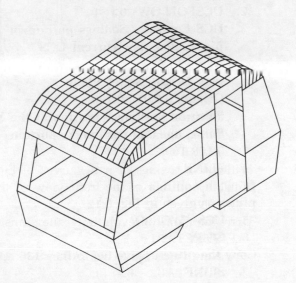

Fig. 6.11 VPOINT view of a
caravan body shell

Figure 6.11 shows the shell of a caravan drawn with the aid of 3DFACEs and the surface command EDGSURF. This Work Example is only concerned with the drawing of the roof of the caravan to demonstrate an example of the command. A later Work Example shows how the roof could also be drawn with the aid of another surface command RULSURF.

Work Example 6/6

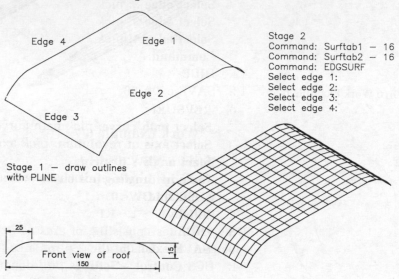

Edge 4   Edge 1

Edge 2

Edge 3

Stage 1 – draw outlines with PLINE

Stage 2
Command: Surftab1 – 16
Command: Surftab2 – 16
Command: EDGSURF
Select edge 1:
Select edge 2:
Select edge 3:
Select edge 4:

25

Front view of roof
150

15

Fig. 6.12 Work Example 6/6

1. **Begin a NEW drawing**
   Enter name of drawing: ex06_06
2. **UCSFOLLOW<0>:** 1
3. **UCS Control – Settings** *pull-down*
   pick **Define new current UCS**
   Name PLAN
   pick **Origin, Xaxis, Plane**
   Origin<0,0,0>: 0,100
   Point on positive-Y portion of the X-axis: 0,400
   Point on the positive-Y portion of the UCS X-Y plane: 0,100,100
4. **PLINE**
Draw the outline of the front view of the roof with arc and line plines as given in Fig. 6.12
5. **UCS *WORLD***
6. **COPY**
Copy the pline to give two plines 130 apart
7. **PLINE**

Join the ends of the two plines with pline lines (as in Fig. 6.12)

8. **VPOINT** −1,−1,1
9. **SURFTAB1**
   New value for SURFTAB1 <6>: 16
10. **SURFTAB2 <6>:**
    New value for SURFTAB2 <6>: 16
11. **EDGESURF**
    Select edge 1: *pick*
    Select edge 2: *pick*
    Select edge 3: *pick*
    Select edge 4: *pick*
    Command:
12. **HIDE**
13. **SAVE** ex06_06

Work Example 6/7

1. **Begin a NEW drawing**
   Name of drawing: ex06_07
2. **UCSFOLLOW<0>:** 1
3. **PLINE**

Draw 2 plines consisting of arcs as in Fig. 6.13. The coordinates given are the ends of the 3 pline arcs making up each pline.

4. **UCS Control – Settings** *pull-down*
   pick **Define new current UCS**
   Name LEFT
   pick **Origin, Xaxis, Plane**

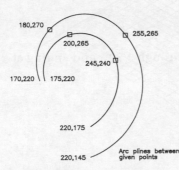

Fig. 6.13 First stage of Work Example 6/7

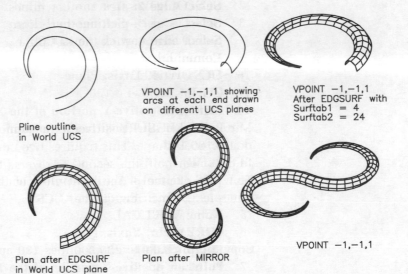

Pline outline in World UCS

VPOINT −1,−1,1 showing arcs at each end drawn on different UCS planes

VPOINT −1,−1,1 After EDGSURF with Surftab1 = 4 Surftab2 = 24

Plan after EDGSURF in World UCS plane

Plan after MIRROR

VPOINT −1,−1,1

Fig. 6.14 Work Example 6/7

Origin<0,0,0>: 170,220
Point on positive-Y portion of the X-axis: 175,220
Point on the positive-Y portion of the UCS X-Y plane: 170,220,100

5. **ZOOM** 1
6. **PLINE**

Draw a pline arc starting at 0,0 passing through 2,2 and ending at 5,0

7. **UCS** *WORLD*
8. **UCS Control – Settings** *pull-down*
    pick **Define new current UCS**
    Name RIGHTEND
    pick **Origin, Xaxis, Plane**
    Origin<0,0,0>: 220,175
    Point on positive-Y portion of the X-axis: 220,145
    Point on the positive-Y portion of the UCS X-Y plane: 220,170,100
9. **ZOOM** 1
10. **PLINE**

Draw a pline arc starting at 0,0 passing through 15,15 and ending at 30,0

11. **UCS** *WORLD*
12. **VPOINT** −1,−1,1
13. **SURFTAB1** <6>: *Ret*
14. **SURFTAB2** <6>: 30
15. **EDGSURF**
    Select edge 1: *pick* one of the plines
    Select edge 2: *pick* another plines
    Select edge 3: *pick* another pline
    Select edge 4: *pick* the last pline
    Command:
16. **UCS** *WORLD*
17. **ZOOM** All
18. **MIRROR**

Mirror the EDGSURF surface in a window to produce the vertical double hook shape. This requires two mirrors – one from the upper to the lower half; the second to reverse the lower half.

19. **UCS Control – Settings** *pull-down*
    pick **Define new current UCS**
    Name VERTICAL
    pick **Origin, Xaxis, Plane**
    Origin<0,0,0>: 220,300
    Point on positive-Y portion of the X-axis: 220,10

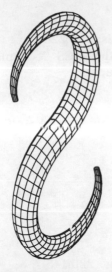

Point on the positive-Y portion of the UCS X-Y plane: 220,300,100

20. **ZOOM** 1
21. **MIRROR**
Mirror the model in a window to produce the lower half of the complete hook.
22. **ROTATE**
Rotate the whole in a window to place the hook in a vertical position (Fig. 6.15).
23. **UCS *WORLD***
24. **VPOINT** −1,−1,1
25. **HIDE**
26. **SAVE** ex06_07

Fig. 6.15 VPOINT view of
Work Example 6/7

Work Example 6/8

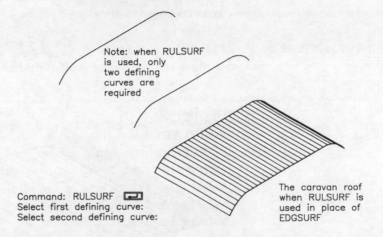

Note: when RULSURF is used, only two defining curves are required

Command: RULSURF
Select first defining curve:
Select second defining curve:

The caravan roof when RULSURF is used in place of EDGSURF

Fig. 6.16 Work Example 6/8

1. **Begin a NEW drawing**
   Enter name of drawing: **ex06_08**
2. **UCSFOLLOW<0>:** 1
3. **UCS Control – Settings** *pull-down*
   pick **Define new current UCS**
   Name PLAN
   pick **Origin, Xaxis, Plane**
   Origin<0,0,0>: 0,100
   Point on positive-Y portion of the X-axis: 0,400
   Point on the positive-Y portion of the UCS X-Y plane: 0,100,100
4. **PLINE**
   Draw the front view pline of the caravan roof again (from Fig. 6.12)

5. **UCS Control – Settings** *pull-down*
pick ***WORLD***
6. **COPY**
Copy the pline to give two plines 130 units apart
7. **VPOINT** −1,−1,1
8. **RULESURF**
   Select first defining curve: *pick*
   Select second defining curve: *pick*
   Command:
9. **SAVE** ex06_08

Work Example 6/9

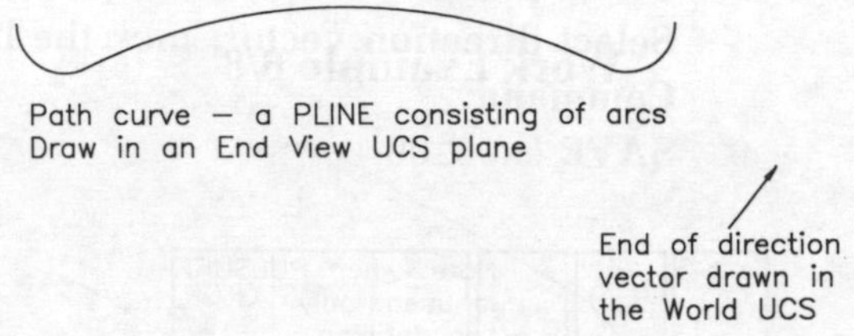

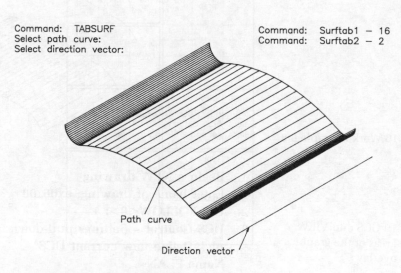

Path curve — a PLINE consisting of arcs
Draw in an End View UCS plane

End of direction
vector drawn in
the World UCS

Fig. 6.17 First stage of Work
Example 6/9

Command: TABSURF
Select path curve:
Select direction vector:

Command: Surftab1 − 16
Command: Surftab2 − 2

Path curve

Direction vector

Fig. 6.18 Work Example 6/9

1. **Begin a NEW drawing**
   Enter name of drawing: ex06_09
2. **UCSFOLLOW<0>:** 1
3. **UCS Control – Settings** *pull-down*
   pick **Define new current UCS**
   Name PLAN
   pick **Origin, Xaxis, Plane**

Origin<0,0,0>: 0,100
Point on positive-Y portion of the X-axis: 0,400
Point on the positive-Y portion of the UCS X-Y plane:
0,100,100

4. **PLINE**

Draw a pline such as that given in Fig. 6.17

5. **LINE**

From point: 200,250 (say)
To point: 200,250,−120 (say)

Any line will do providing it is not parallel with the pline

6. **UCS *WORLD***
7. **VPOINT** −1,−1,1
8. **TABSURF**

Select path curve: *pick the pline*
Select direction vector: *pick the line*
Command:

9. **SAVE** ex06_09

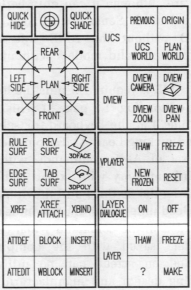

Fig. 6.19 UCS and VIEW
menu areas of the graphics
tablet overlay

SHADE/VIEW/UCS/BLOCKS/LAYERS

CHAPTER 7

The AutoCAD Advanced Modeling Extension

Introduction

This chapter outlines the Advanced Modeling Extension (AME) facility, first introduced as an optional extension for AutoCAD Release 11. AME is for producing 3D solid models with AutoCAD. The AME software is a separate package from the AutoCAD Release 11 software, although it can only be loaded when AutoCAD itself has been loaded. Some of the AME facilities are available with AutoCAD without the AME software being loaded, but the construction of solid models without the full AME is somewhat limited.

When AME is required it must be loaded while in the AutoCAD drawing editor (Fig. 1.2 page 2). This is achieved either by typing (xload "ame") at the keyboard, or selecting the Solids pull-down menu and picking Load AME from the menu when it appears. The limited set of AME commands within AutoCAD must also be loaded into memory with (xload "amelite") or by selecting Load amelite from the Settings pull-down menu. Note that the AME files will not load unless both the parentheses and the inverted commas are included in the command when typed at the keyboard.

The data saved with the computer files of solid models constructed on screen can be utilised in other areas of the engineering design and manufacturing process. Stored with the data in the drawing file will be details of the physical and material properties of the model. Details such as surface area, mass, volume, physical properties related to various materials can be assessed from the files for analysis of the model. The data can be utilised for the construction of 2D orthographic projections or for computer numerical control (CNC) of machinery and for other features of engineering design and manufacture.

AME solid models are constructed under the control of a set of commands. There are three ways in which solid models can be constructed with the aid of AME.

1. By joining together, by subtracting from or by the intersection of a group of basic 'building blocks'. These are the geometrical solids – BOX, WEDGE, CYLINDER, CONE, SPHERE and TORUS. These operations utilise the Boolean operators – join, difference (subtraction) and intersect.
2. By the extrusion of 2D outlines constructed mainly with PLINE and CIRCLE. This extrusion facility adds height to the 2D outline.
3. By the revolving of 2D shapes around a central axis. This produces what are generally referred to as 2½D solids.

AME models appear on screen as wireframes. These can be surface meshed to produce models which can be shaded and which can be acted upon to have hidden lines behind faces removed.

AME commands

There are several ways in which the AME commands can be called.

1. By typing the commands – which all begin with SOL, in full at the command line – e.g. SOLBOX brings the command for determining the size, shape and position of the geometrical box solid.
2. If a standard AutoCAD Release 11 software is installed in the computer being used, a file *acad. pgp* will be present. This file allows abbreviations to be used in place of the full SOL command. Thus BOX will call the command rather than SOLBOX.
3. All the AME commands can be selected from the SOLIDS on-screen sub-menus by pointing with the aid of the selection device (mouse, puck, stylus).
4. All the SOL commands can also be picked from the SOLIDS pull-down menu and its sub-menus.
5. All the AME commands can be selected from the standard AutoCAD Release 11 graphics tablet overlay – top left corner of the menu areas – as shown in Fig. 7.18 (page 157).

The AME primitives

The six AME primitive solids are shown in Fig. 7.2. The commands and prompts appearing at the command line of the AutoCAD drawing editor when each of these solids is to be constructed are given in Fig. 7.2. The sequences of prompts for each command are given below. Note that following the last prompt in each example,

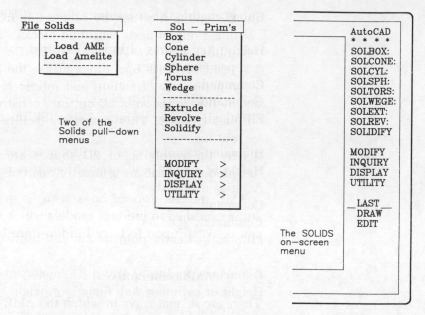

Fig. 7.1 The SOLIDS
pull-down menu and
SOLIDS on-screen menu

AutoCAD informs the user of the stages of the operation of forming the solid with messages appearing at the command line. These messages are not given here.

Note: The solids given in the drawings of Fig. 7.2 have been placed in a pictorial view with the aid of the command VPOINT set at −1,−1,1.

Command: SOLBOX
Corner of box: *pick* or *Key* coordinates

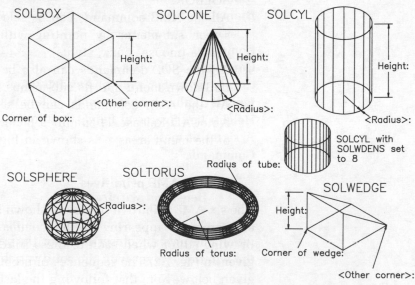

Fig. 7.2 The six AME
primitives

Cube/Length/<Other corner>: *Key* c (CUBE), l (Length) or give coordinates

Height: *Key* figures of height required

A series of messages

Command:

Command: SOLCONE

Elliptical/<Center point>: *Key* e (Elliptical) or coordinates of centre point

Diameter/<Radius>: *Key* d (Diameter) or coordinates of Radius

Height of cone: *Key* figures of height required

A series of messages

Command:

Command: SOLCYL

Elliptical/<Center point>: *Key* e (Elliptical) or coordinates of centre point

Diameter/<Radius>: *Key* d (Diameter) or coordinates of Radius

Height of cylinder: *Key* figures of height required

A series of messages

Command:

Command: SOLSPHERE

Center of sphere: *pick* or *Key* figures of coordinates

Diameter/<Radius> of sphere: *Key* figures of height required

A series of messages

Command:

Command: SOLTORUS

Center of torus: *pick* or *Key* figures of coordinates

Diameter/<Radius> of torus: *pick* or *Key* figures of coordinates

Diameter/<Radius> of tube: *pick* or *Key* figures of coordinates

A series of messages

Command:

Command: SOLWEDGE

Corner of wedge: *pick* or *Key* figures of coordinates

Length/<Other corner>: *pick* or *Key* figures of coordinates

Height: *Key* figures of height required

A series of messages

Command:

Density of wireframes

Note: In Fig. 7.2 a second solid cylinder is shown in which the wireframe mesh is closer than for the other solids. The density of the wireframe is set with the solid variable SOLWDENS as follows:

Command: SOLWDENS
Wireframe mesh density (1 to 8) <4>: 8 *Key Ret*
A series of messages
Command:

Forming a solid mesh

Figure 7.3 shows the solids after they have been meshed and then had hidden lines removed. The procedure is as follows:

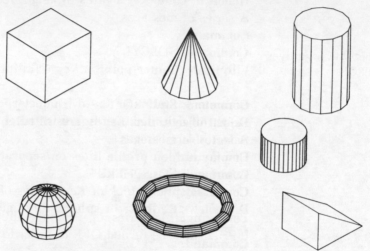

Fig. 7.3 The AME primitives after HIDE

Command: SOLMESH
Select solids to be meshed...
Select solids: *pick the solid(s)* **1 selected, 1 found**
Select solids: *Ret*
A series of messages
Command:
Command: HIDE *Ret*
HIDE Regenerating drawing
Removing hidden lines: 1250 (say)
Command:

Forming a solid profile

Figure 7.4 shows the same solids after the command SOLPROF (solid profile) has been in action. It must be noted here that solid profile views from AME are specific to the chosen view. If the viewing point is changed it will be seen that some of the profile lines will be incorrect or missing. The procedure for obtaining a profile view of an AME solid model is:

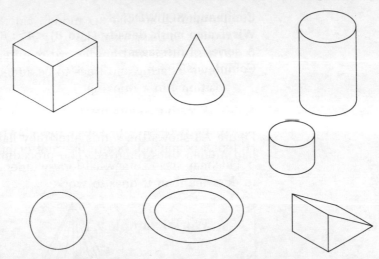

Fig. 7.4 The AME primitives
after SOLPROF

Command: SOLPROF
Select objects: *pick* solids **1 selected, 1 found**
Select objects: *Ret*
Display hidden profile lines on separate layer ? <N>: y (Yes)
A series of messages
Command:

Following this series of prompts and responses, Layers 0 and
0-PH-2 must be turned OFF in order to obtain the required profile
on screen.

Note about titles and borders to Work Examples

AME is designed for producing solid models in 3D space. 3D Solid
models cannot be drawn when in PSPACE. VPOINT views of 3D
models cannot be produced when in PSPACE.

It may be necessary to combine VPOINT pictorial views of a 3D
model with a title and borders in a drawing. It may also be
necessary to use HIDE to remove hidden lines from a 3D model.
These are possible by working as follows:

1. Set TILEMODE to 0 (OFF). This automatically places the
    drawing editor into PSPACE. 3D models disappear from the
    screen.
2. Call the command MVIEW for setting viewports. If only one
    viewport is required, answer the MVIEW prompts with f (Fit).
    Any 3D models reappear.
3. Set UCSFOLLOW to 1 (ON). If a new UCS plane is set, the
    screen will follow the setting.

4. To manipulate the 3D model, call MSPACE. This allows 3D models to be worked on.

5. When a title and border are required revert to PSPACE. This allows lettering and lines to be added horizontally (or in other positions) to a drawing.

However, note that to HIDE hidden lines when plotting or printing, it will be necessary to select the viewports(s) using the MVIEW Hideplot command, before the plot or print commences.

This may seem somewhat long-winded, but in fact it takes longer to describe than it does to work.

Work Example 7/1

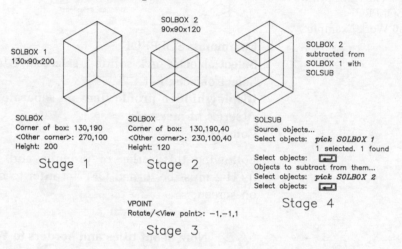

SOLBOX 1
130x90x200

SOLBOX 2
90x90x120

SOLBOX 2
subtracted from
SOLBOX 1 with
SOLSUB

SOLBOX
Corner of box: 130,190
<Other corner>: 270,100
Height: 200

Stage 1

SOLBOX
Corner of box: 130,190,40
<Other corner>: 230,100,40
Height: 120

Stage 2

SOLSUB
Source objects...
Select objects: *pick SOLBOX 1*
    1 selected. 1 found
Select objects: ⏎
Objects to subtract from them...
Select objects: *pick SOLBOX 2*
Select objects: ⏎

Stage 4

VPOINT
Rotate/<View point>: −1,−1,1

Stage 3

Fig. 7.5 Work Example 7/1

Follow the stages described in Fig. 7.5, by keying the various commands and answers to prompts as shown. This is an example of the use of the command **SOLSUB** in which one AME solid object is subtracted from another.

Work Example 7/2

Follow the stages described in Fig. 7.6, by keying the commands and responses to prompts as shown. This is an example of the command SOLUNION in which three AME solid models are joined to each other.

Work Example 7/3

Follow the stages described in Fig. 7.7, by keying the commands

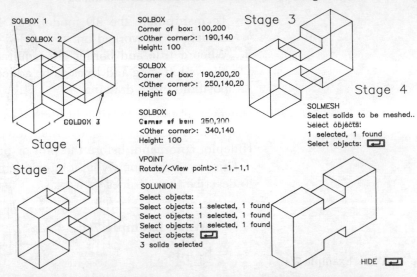

SOLBOX
Corner of box: 100,200
<Other corner>: 190,140
Height: 100

SOLBOX
Corner of box: 190,200,20
<Other corner>: 250,140,20
Height: 60

SOLBOX
Corner of box: 250,200
<Other corner>: 340,140
Height: 100

VPOINT
Rotate/<View point>: −1,−1,1

SOLUNION
Select objects:
Select objects: 1 selected, 1 found
Select objects: 1 selected, 1 found
Select objects: 1 selected, 1 found
Select objects: ⏎
3 solids selected

SOLMESH
Select solids to be meshed..
Select objects:
1 selected, 1 found
Select objects: ⏎

Stage 1

Stage 2

Stage 3

Stage 4

HIDE ⏎

Fig. 7.6 Work Example 7/2

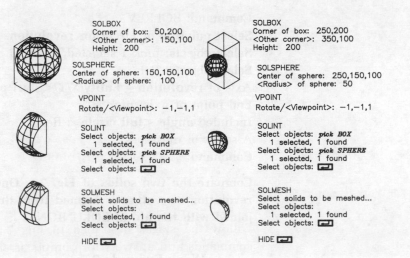

SOLBOX
Corner of box: 50,200
<Other corner>: 150,100
Height: 200

SOLSPHERE
Center of sphere: 150,150,100
<Radius> of sphere: 100

VPOINT
Rotate/<Viewpoint>: −1,−1,1

SOLINT
Select objects: *pick BOX*
    1 selected, 1 found
Select objects: *pick SPHERE*
    1 selected, 1 found
Select objects: ⏎

SOLMESH
Select solids to be meshed...
Select objects:
    1 selected, 1 found
Select objects: ⏎

HIDE ⏎

SOLBOX
Corner of box: 250,200
<Other corner>: 350,100
Height: 200

SOLSPHERE
Center of sphere: 250,150,100
<Radius> of sphere: 50

VPOINT
Rotate/<Viewpoint>: −1,−1,1

SOLINT
Select objects: *pick BOX*
    1 selected, 1 found
Select objects: *pick SPHERE*
    1 selected, 1 found
Select objects: ⏎

SOLMESH
Select solids to be meshed...
Select objects:
    1 selected, 1 found
Select objects: ⏎

HIDE ⏎

Fig. 7.7 Work Example 7/3

and responses to prompts as shown. This is an example of the command SOLINT in which three AME solid models are made to intersect with each other.

Work Example 7/4

Follow the stages described in Fig. 7.8, by keying the commands and responses to prompts as shown. This gives an example of the command SOLREV in which three AME solid models are formed by solids of revolution and then acted upon by the two commands SOLSUB and SOLUNION. The process of forming a solid of revolution takes the form:

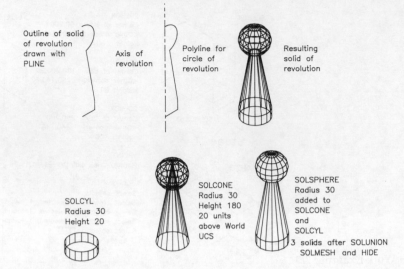

Fig. 7.8 Work Example 7/4

Command: SOLREV
Select polyline or circle for revolution. . .
Select objects: *pick* **1 selected, 1 found**
Select objects: *Ret*
Axis of revolution – Entity/X/Y/<Start point of axis>: *pick*
End point of axis: *pick*
Included angle <full circle>: *Ret*
A series of messages
Command:

Compare the two solids of Fig. 7.8. One is formed as a solid of revolution, the other is formed from three AME solid primitives joined with the aid of SOLUNION.

Work Example 7/5

Stage 1 (Fig. 7.9)
1. **1. Begin a NEW drawing** – Main Menu
        Enter name of drawing ex07_05
2. (xload "ame")
3. **Command:** SOLBOX (1st solbox)
        Corner of box: 110,220
        <Other corner>: 300,130
        Height: 30
4. **Command:** SOLBOX (2nd solbox)
        Corner of box: 140,220,30
        <Other corner>: 170,130,30

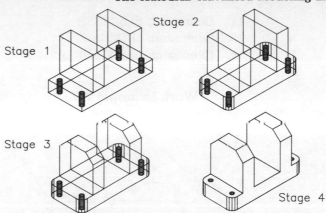

Fig. 7.9 Work Example 7/5

Height: 90

5. **Command:** COPY
   Copy SOLBOX 2 to new second position
6. **Command:** SOLCYL
   <Center point>: 125,205
   <Radius>: 5
   Height of cylinder: 30
7. **Command:** COPY
   Copy the solcylinder to 3 other positions
8. **Command:** VPOINT −1,−1,1
9. **Command:** ZOOM   Zoom window the solid as large as possible

Stage 2 (Fig. 7.9)

10. **Command:** SOLFILL
    Select edges to be filleted: *pick* the four edges
    4 edges selected.
    <Radius> of fillet: 15

Stage 3 (Fig. 7.9)

11. **Command:** SOLCHAM
    Select base surface: *pick* surface
    <OK>Next: *Key* n (next) as necessary, then *Ret*
    Select edges to be chamfered: *pick*
    Chamfer distance: 20
    Second chamfer distance: 20

    Note: It will probably be necessary to pick at least two faces by keying n (Next) at the OK<Next>: prompt.

12. **Command:** SOLSUB
Subtract cylinders from base
13. **Command:** SOLUNION
Select all three solids

14. **Command:** SOLMESH
15. **Command:** HIDE
16. **Command:** SAVE ex07_05

Work Example 7/6

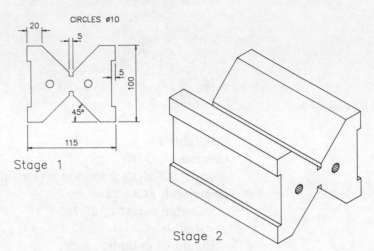

Stage 1

Stage 2

Fig. 7.10 Work Example 7/6

1. **1. NEW drawing**
   Name of drawing: ex07_06
2. **Command:** (xload "ame")
3. **Command:** UCSFOLLOW<<0>: 1
4. **UCS CONTROL – Settings**
   pick **Define new current UCS**
   Name PLAN
   pick **Origin, Xaxis, Plane**
   Origin point<0,0,0>: 0,150
   Position on positive portion of X-axis: 420,150
   Point on positive-Y portion of the UCS X-Y plane: 0,150,100

Note: This causes the UCS to change from World to Plan view.

5. **Command:** ZOOM 1

Note: When wishing to draw in the World UCS, pick the UCS Control from the Settings pull-down menu and select *WORLD* from the dialogue box which appears. When wishing to draw in the Plan UCS select PLAN from the UCS dialogue box.

6. In the PLAN UCS construct the drawing Stage 1 (Fig. 7.6) with PLINE and CIRCLE
7. **Command:** SOLEXT
   Select polylines and circles for extrusion. . .
   Select objects: *pick* **1 selected, 1 found**

        Select objects: *pick* **1 selected, 1 found**
        Select objects: *pick* **1 selected, 1 found**
        Select objects: *Ret*
        Height of extrusion: 150
        Extrusion taper angle from Z<0>: *Ret*

8. **UCS CONTROL – Settings**
    select *WORLD*
9. **Command:** ZOOM 1
10. **Command:** VPOINT −1,−1,1
11. **Command:** SOLSUB

Subtract cylinders from extrusion block

12. **Command:** SOLMESH
13. **Command:** HIDE
14. **Command:** SAVE ex07_06

Work Example 7/7

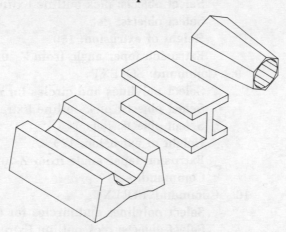

Fig. 7.11 Work Example 7/7

1. **1, NEW drawing – Main Menu**
    Name of drawing: ex07_07
2. **Command:** (xload "ame")
3. **Command:** UCSFOLLOW<<0>: 1
4. **UCS CONTROL – Settings**
    pick **Define new current UCS**
    Name PLAN
    pick **Origin, Xaxis, Plane**
    Origin point<0,0,0>: 0,150
    Position on positive portion of X-axis: 420,150
    Point on positive-Y portion of the UCS X-Y plane: 0,150,100
5. **Command:** PLINE

Copy the polyline outlines Extrusion 1 and Extrusion 2 of Fig. 7.11

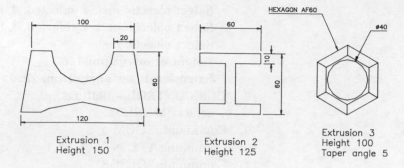

Fig. 7.12 First stage of Work
Example 7/7

Extrusion 1
Height 150

Extrusion 2
Height 125

Extrusion 3
Height 100
Taper angle 5

6. **Command:** POLYGON
Draw the polygon of Extrusion 3 of Fig. 7.12
7. **Command:** CIRCLE
Draw the circle of Extrusion 3 of Fig. 7.12
8. **Command:** SOLEXT
    Select polylines and circles for extrusion. . .
    Select objects: *pick* outline Extrusion 1 **1 selected, 1 found**
    Select objects: *Ret*
    Height of extrusion: 150
    Extrusion taper angle from Z<0>: *Ret*
9. **Command:** SOLEXT
    Select polylines and circles for extrusion. . .
    Select objects: *pick* outline Extrusion 2 **1 selected, 1 found**
    Select objects: *Ret*
    Height of extrusion: 125
    Extrusion taper angle from Z<0>: *Ret*
    Command:
10. **Command:** SOLEXT
    Select polylines and circles for extrusion. . .
    Select objects: *pick* outline Extrusion 3 **1 selected, 1 found**
    Select objects: *Ret*
    Height of extrusion: 100
    Extrusion taper angle from Z<0>: 5
    Command:
11. **UCS Control – Settings**
    pick ***WORLD***
12. **Command:** VPOINT −1,−1,1
13. **Command:** SOLSUB
Subtract the circle (cylinder) extrusion from the polygon extrusion
14. **Command:** SOLMESH
    Select solids to be meshed. . .
    Select solids: *pick* Extrusion 1 **1 selected, 1 found**
    Select solids: *pick* Extrusion 2 **1 selected, 1 found**

Select solids: *pick* Extrusion 3 **1 selected, 1 found**
Select solids: *Ret*
A series of messages
Command:
15. **Command:** HIDE
16. **Command:** SAVE ex07_07

Work Example 7/8

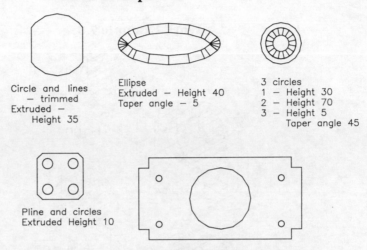

Circle and lines
— trimmed
Extruded —
Height 35

Ellipse
Extruded — Height 40
Taper angle — 5

3 circles
1 — Height 30
2 — Height 70
3 — Height 5
    Taper angle 45

Pline and circles
Extruded Height 10

Pline and circles   Extrude height 5

Fig. 7.14 First stage of Work
Example 7/8

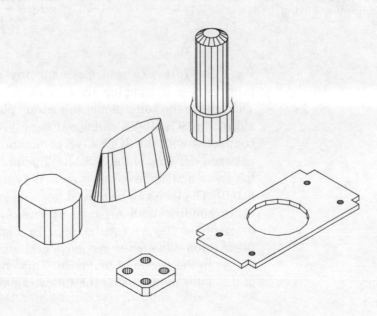

Fig. 7.13 Work Example 7/8

This Work Example follows the same procedures as for Work Example 7/7. It is included here to give the reader further work in producing solid model extrusions. Note the plan views must be drawn in a WORLD UCS. See item 5 of Work Example 7/7. The viewing of the extrusions from a VPOINT can only be carried out if the UCS is returned to its World position. However, try the VPOINT viewing position from the PLAN UCS.

Work Example 7/9

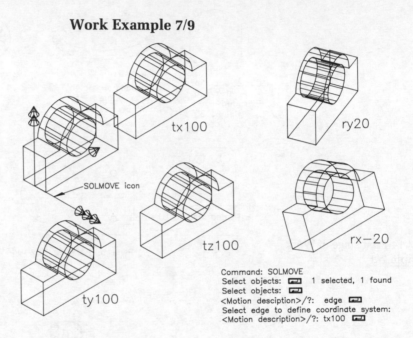

Fig. 7.15 Examples of using SOLMOVE

```
Command: SOLMOVE
Select objects: ⬜  1 selected, 1 found
Select objects: ⬜
<Motion desciption>/?:   edge ⬜
Select edge to define coordinate system:
<Motion description>/?: tx100 ⬜
```

For this Work Example make up any solid model from several primitives and combine them with SOLUNION and/or SOLSUB. Then move the solid model to various positions on screen with the aid of the SOLMOVE command facility. The sequence of prompts connected with the SOLMOVE command are given in Fig. 7.15. An enlarged drawing of the SOLMOVE icon is given in Fig. 7.16. When the icon first appears on screen it is at the UCS origin, usually (0,0,0). The icon can be moved to an edge or a face of a solid model by responding with e (edge) or f (face) to the prompt <Motion description>/?:. As can be seen in Fig. 7.15, when the Motion description edge is the response and an edge is selected, the icon moves to the centre of that edge. This enables accurate positioning of the solid model using the following abbreviations:

t – transfer in a straight line

r – rotate

Examples of the action of these Motion abbreviations are shown in Fig. 7.15. Figure 7.16 shows the directions of movement or the axes of rotation of the three arms of the SOLMOVE icon.

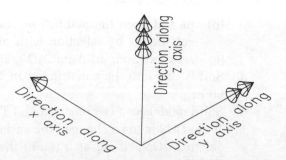

Fig. 7.16 The SOLMOVE icon

Work Example 7/10

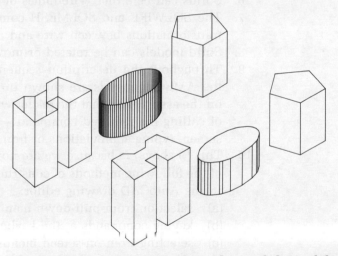

Fig. 7.17 Extrusions drawn with SOLEXTRUDE and the same extrusions after SOLIDIFY

Figure 7.17 gives examples of 3 solid models formed from extrusions drawn with the aid of the ELEVATION command. Such extrusions can be made into AME solids with the SOLIDIFY command, followed by the SOLMESH. Practise this facility with examples such as those given in Fig. 7.17.

Notes on the use of the Advanced Modelling Extension

1. It will have been noted that all the AME commands begin with SOL.
2. Solid models can be constructed with the aid of the AME

command systems, which can be called as follows:

(a) from the Solids pull-down menu or its sub-menus;

(b) typed in full – e.g. SOLBOX at the command line;

(c) if standard Release 11 AutoCAD software is installed, it will contain a file acad.pgp, which will allow AME SOL commands to be abbreviated – e.g. CYL for SOLCYLINDER;

(d) picked from the SOLIDS on-screen menu and associated sub-menus by selection with mouse, puck or stylus;

(e) selected from an AutoCAD graphics tablet overlay.

3. Solids can only be constructed in MSPACE if TILEMODE is OFF.

4. Solid models can be constructed if TILEMODE is ON (set at 1).

5. If the UCS is to be changed the variable UCSFOLLOW must be set to 1 (ON). If set at 0 (OFF) the UCS can only be in the WORLD position and any changes in the UCS will not follow on the given commands.

6. Solids can be either Wireframes or Meshes.

7. The SOLWIRE and SOLMESH commands are used for these transformations between wire and mesh.

8. Solid models can be rotated or moved with SOLMOVE.

9. Throughout the description sequences given in this chapter the AME commands are shown in the form, e.g., SOLCONE, on the assumption that the reader will choose his own method of calling the required command – from pull-down, from on-screen, typing abbreviations or from a graphics tablet overlay.

10. This (9 above) is because we are now in a position to use any of the following methods of constructing drawings and models in the AutoCAD drawing editor:

(a) selection from pull-down menus and sub-menus;

(b) keying commands at the keyboard;

(c) selecting from on-screen menus and sub-menus;

(d) selecting from a graphics tablet overlay;

(e) selecting with a mouse, puck or stylus;

(f) using mouse, puck, stylus or types numbers to determine positions of the ends of objects drawn in the drawing editor.

11. In the above descriptions, commands and responses to prompts have been shown as if typed in at the keyboard, unless shown as being picked. It is assumed that by now readers will understand that details typed at the keyboard will normally be followed by pressing the Return key of the

computer. Therefore the Ret statement (for pressing the Return key) is not included in the steps given throughout this chapter – unless Ret is necessary without having first typed a command or a response.

12. Note that the prompts which occur with commands from AME are, at times, rather complex. In the sequences given above only the barely necessary prompts have been included. The messages showing the stages at which the AME software is completing its tasks are shown by the statement 'A series of messages'.

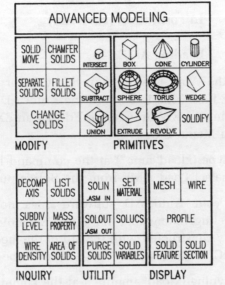

Fig. 7.18 The AME menu areas of the graphics tablet overlay

CHAPTER 8

The Advanced Modeling Extension

Introduction (revision)

Loading AME

All the Work Examples in this chapter require the loading of the AME files. This is done in the AutoCAD drawing editor – i.e. after naming a NEW drawing or Editing an EXISTING drawing from the Main Menu. Either:

1. type (xload"ame") at the command line – or –
2. select Load AME from the Solids pull-down menu.

If your AutoCAD software does not include the Advanced Modeling Extension, the Work Examples in this chapter can be partly constructed with the aid of the modelling files supplied with AutoCAD Release 11. These files can be loaded by:

1. typing (xload"amelite") at the command line – or –
2. selecting Load Amelite from the Solids pull-down menu.

AME commands

When a command such as SOLBOX is required, it can be called in one of several ways:

1. by keying SOLBOX at the keyboard;
2. by keying its abbreviation BOX, if the file acad.pgp is present with the AutoCAD software files;
3. by selecting Primitives from the Solids pull-down menu and then further selecting Box from the resulting Sol – Prim's sub-menu;
4. by selecting SOLIDS from the AutoCAD on-screen menu and then SOLBOX from the resulting Solids menu. This results in a further sub-menu devoted to Solbox prompts;
5. by picking Solbox from a graphics tablet overlay.

Coordinates

The coordinates given in the Work Examples may either be:

1. typed in full at the keyboard, followed by pressing the Return key;
2. picked with the aid of a mouse, puck or stylus;
3. if a z coordinate is required, it can be either:
   (a) typed with the x,y coordinates;
   (b) by typing .XY, then typing or picking the x,y coordinates, followed by typing the z coordinate when (need Z) appears as a prompt;
   (c) picking .XY from the Filters pull-down menu, followed by typing (or picking) the x,y coordinates and then typing the z coordinate when (need Z): appears as a prompt.

Minimal sequence descriptions

In the Work Examples in this chapter, descriptions of the sequences of operations to be performed are not described as fully as in previous chapters. Only minimal instructions are shown. This is because it is assumed that by now, the reader will be fully conversant with the AutoCAD command and prompts systems.

AME solid drawing files

AME solid model drawing files may be very large, perhaps requiring some hundreds of kilobytes of disk space. Some of the Work Examples in this chapter will need as much as 200 or more kilobytes of disk space. It must be remembered that, if working with a floppy disk of only 360 Kb size, it may only be possible to save a single Work Example to such a disk.

Work Example 8/1

1. **1. Begin a NEW drawing** – Main Menu
   Enter name of drawing: ex08_01
2. (xload"ame") or select **Load AME** from **Solids**
3. **VPOINT1** −1,−1,1
4. **SOLBOX**
Corner of box:	100,210
<Other corner>:	320,190
Height:	100
5. **SOLBOX**

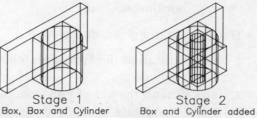

Stage 1
Box, Box and Cylinder

Stage 2
Box and Cylinder added

Stage 3
3 primitives acted
on by Solunion

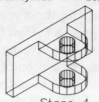
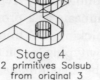

Stage 4
2 primitives Solsub
from original 3

Stage 5
Corners of backplate
Solfilleted

Fig. 8.1 Stages in constructing Work Example 8/1

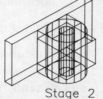

Fig. 8.2 Work Example 8/1

Corner of box:	170,190
<Other corner>:	250,150
Height:	100

6. **SOLCYL**

<Center point>:	210,150
<Radius>:	40
Height of cylinder:	100

Note: These three solid primitives are shown in Stage 1 of Fig. 8.1.

7. **SOLBOX**

Corners 170,190,20 and 250,110,20; **Height** 60

8. **SOLCYLINDER**

<Center point>:	210,150
<Radius>:	15
Height of cylinder:	100

Note: These two solid primitives are shown in Stage 2 of Fig. 8.1.

9. **SOLUNION**

Select the three objects **SOLBOX** item 4, **SOLBOX** item 5 and **SOLCYLINDER** item 6

Note: The union of these three solid primitives is shown in Stage 3 of Fig. 8.1.

10. **SOLSUB**

Objects to subtract from:	*pick* the union just formed
Objects to be subtracted:	*pick* the other two solids

Note: This **SOLSUB** is shown in Stage 4 of Fig. 8.1.

11. **SOLFILLET**

Select edges:	*pick* the 4 corners of the backplate

<**Radius of fillet**>: 15

Note: This filleting is shown in Stage 5 of Fig. 8.1.
12. **SOLMESH**
    Solid objects to be meshed...
    Select objects: *pick* the whole solid model
13. **HIDE**
14. **SAVE** ex08_01

Note: Do not attempt including a title block or a border to this drawing.

Work Example 8/2

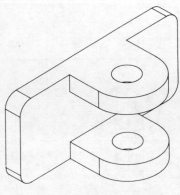

Fig. 8.3 Work Example 8/2

In this Work Example the solid model drawn in Work Example 8/1 will be formed into a profile-only solid with hidden lines removed. Note that such profiles are not true solid models, they are views which are specific to the viewpoint from which they were taken. If another VPOINT is taken, it will be seen that the solid model will be incomplete. If starting this Work Example from computer and AutoCAD startup, it will be necessary to again (xload"ame").
1. **Edit an EXISTING drawing – Main menu**
    Enter name of DRAWING: ex08_01
2. **TILEMODE<1>:** 0 Pspace icon appears
3. **LIMITS**
    <Lower left corner>: <0,0>:*Ret*
    Upper right corner <12,9): 420,297
4. **ZOOM** a (All)
5. **Layer Control – Settings**
Make a new layer VPORTS – colour green. Make VPORTS the current layer
6. **MVIEW**   f (Fit) drawing of model reappears
7. **MSPACE**
8. **SOLPROF**
    Select objects: *pick* the solid model
    Display hidden lines on
    separate layers<N>:   y (Yes)
9. **Layer Control – Settings**
Turn Layers 0 and 0-ph-2 OFF
10. **SAVE** ex08_02
11. **QUIT**   **Really want to discard all changes in drawing?**   y (Yes)
Note: Do not use the command **END** here, because the drawing

would then be saved to the filename ex08_01 – the filename of the drawing originally loaded. The command QUIT discards all changes made to the drawing, but will leave both files ex08_01.dwg and ex08_02.dwg intact.

Work Example 8/3

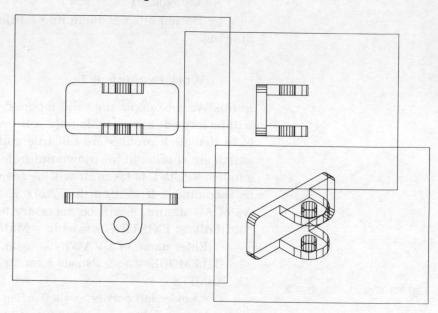

Fig. 8.4 Moving Viewports

1. **Edit an EXISTING drawing – Main Menu**
   Enter name of DRAWING: ex08_01
2. **TILEMODE<1>:** 0 – (drawing disappears and paper space icon appears)
3. **LIMITS** (May not be necessary, but check)
   <Lower left corner>: <0,0>: *Ret*
   Upper right corner <12,9): 420,297
4. **ZOOM** a (All)
5. **Layer Control – Settings**
Make a new layer VPORTS – colour green
6. **MVIEW Fit/2/3/4/Restore//<First Point>:** 4
   Fit/2/3/4: f (Fit)
(Drawing reappears in each of 4 viewports)
7. **MSPACE** (UCS icons reappear in each viewport)
8. Make top left Vport active – move arrow to the viewport and press the *pick* button of the selection device
9. **VPOINT** 0,0,1
10. Make bottom left viewport active

           VPOINT 0,−1,0
11.   Make top right viewport active
           VPOINT −1,−1,1
12.   Make bottom right viewport active
           VPOINT −1,0,0
13.   In each viewport in turn
           ZOOM 1
14.   **PSPACE** (UCS icons disappear; paperspace icon reappears)
15.   **MOVE**
Move each viewport to a suitable position (Fig. 8.4). This involves placing the pick box over one of the lines surrounding the viewport to be moved in response to the Select objects: prompt of the MOVE command. The whole viewport, with its drawing, can then be moved under the control of the selection device
16.   **Layer Control – Settings**
Make Layer 0 the current layer
17.   **LINE**
Add a suitable border and title block
18.   **TEXT**
Add title in **ROMANS** style with text 8 units high
19.   **MVIEW**
           ON/OFF/Hideplot/Fit/2/3/4/Restore/: h (Hideplot)
           ON/OFF: on
           Select objects: *pick* the **edges** of each viewport in turn
20.   **Layer Control – Settings**
Turn Layer VPORTS off
21.   **SAVE** ex08_03
22.   **PLOT** (plot to plotter) or **PRPLOT** (print to printer)

   Note: Hideplot is saved with each viewport. When plotted (or printed) with hide, all hidden lines are removed in each viewport before plotting (or printing) commences. Hideplot can be checked on screen if wished, by calling HIDE while in MSPACE.

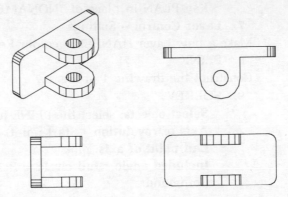

Fig. 8.5 Work Example 8/3

Work Example 8/4

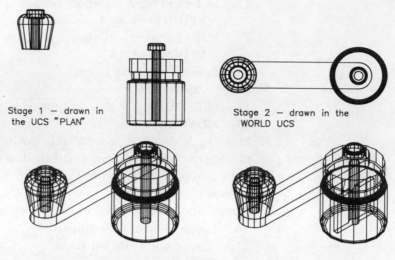

Stage 1 – drawn in the UCS "PLAN"

Stage 2 – drawn in the WORLD UCS

Fig. 8.6 Stages in constructing Work Example 8/4

Stage 2 – as seen with VPOINT: –1,–1,1

Stage 3 – Blade added and Solmesh called

1. **Begin a NEW drawing – Main Menu**
   Enter name of drawing: ex08_04
2. (xload"ame") – if necessary
3. **UCSFOLLOW<0>:** 1
4. **UCS**
   Origin/ZAxis/3point/Entity/View/X/Y/Z/Prev/Restore/Save/ Del/?/<World>: 3 (3point)
   Origin point<0,0,0): 0,100
   Point on portion of the X-axis<1,0,0>: 420,100
   Point on positive-Y portion of the UCS X-Y plane <0,1,0): 0,100,100
5. **ZOOM** All (important in this Example at this stage)
6. **UCS Control – Settings**
   Key PLAN in place of ***NONAME***
7. **Layer Control – Settings**
   Make a new Layer HANDLE – colour Red
8. **PLINE**
   Construct the drawing 1 of Fig. 8.7
9. **SOLREV**
   Select objects: select the PLINE just drawn
   Axis of revolution <Start point>: *pick*
   End point of axis: *pick*
   Included angle <full circle>: *Ret*
   Command:

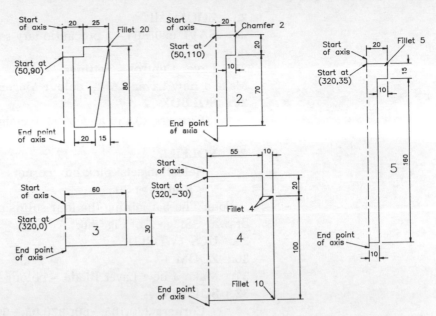

Fig. 8.7 SOLREV outlines for Work Example 8/4

10. Make a new Layer PIN – colour Yellow
11. **PLINE**
Draw outline Drawing 2 of Fig. 8.7
12. **SOLREV**
Make last drawn PLINE a solid of revolution
13. Make a new Layer LID – colour Green
14. **PLINE**
Draw outline Drawing 3 of Fig. 8.7
15. **SOLREV**
Make last drawn PLINE a solid of revolution
16. Make a new Layer BOTTLE – colour Cyan
17. **PLINE**
Draw outline Drawing 4 of Fig. 8.7
18. **SOLREV**
Make last drawn PLINE a solid of revolution
19. Make a new Layer PIN2 – colour Blue
20. **PLINE**
Draw outline Drawing 5 of Fig. 8.7
21. **SOLREV**
Make last drawn PLINE a solid of revolution
   Note: The first stages of drawing the five solids of revolution shown in Fig. 8.6 have now been constructed in the UCS PLAN.
22. **UCS Control – Settings**
       Select ***WORLD***

23. **ZOOM** All
24. **SAVE** ex08_04 – a precautionary save to avoid loss of drawing data
25. **Layer Control – Settings**
Make a new Layer BAR – colour Magenta
26. **SOLBOX**
       Corners 20,130 and 350,70; **Height** 20
27. **VPOINT** −1,−1,1
28. **SOLFILL**
       Select objects: *pick* box corners
       <Radius>: 30
  Note: The bar joining the four solids of revolution has now been drawn – Stage 2 of Fig. 8.6.
29. **UCS** *WORLD*
30. **ZOOM** 1
31. Make a new Layer Blade – colour White
32. **SOLBOX**
       Corners 270,105,−60; 370,95,−60; **Height** −80
33. **VPOINT** −1,−1,1
34. **ZOOM** w (window)
Enlarge model to fill screen
  Note: The completed solid model has now been drawn – Stage 3 of Fig. 8.6.
35. **SOLUNION**
Select PIN, BAR, PIN2 and BLADE
36. **SOLMESH**
Select each of the solid objects – the SOLUNION (item 35), the BOTTLE, HANDLE and LID in turn
37. **HIDE**
38. **SAVE** ex08_04 – precautionary save
39. **SHADE** – try out this command
40. **REGEN** – revert to previous screen before SHADE

Work Example 8/5

1. **Edit an EXISTING drawing – Main Menu**
       Enter NAME of drawing: ex08_04
2. **TILEMODE<1>:** 0
3. **Layer Control – Settings**
Make layer VPORTS colour yellow
4. **LIMITS**
Set limits to 0,0 and 420,297
5. **ZOOM** All

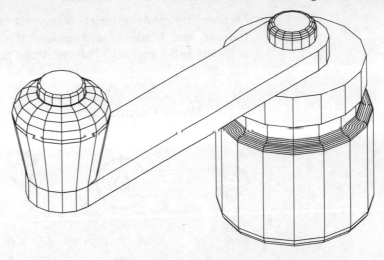

Fig. 8.8 Work Example 8/4
after HIDE

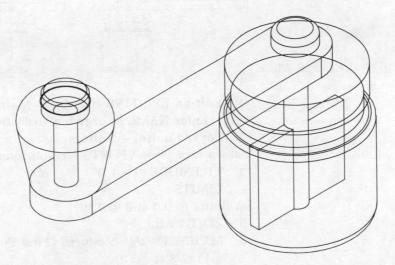

Fig. 8.9 Work Example 8/5

6. **MVIEW**
   F (Fit)
7. **MSPACE**
8. **SOLPROF**
   Select objects: *pick* the SOLUNION
   Select objects: *pick* the BOTTLE
   Select objects: *pick* the HANDLE
   Select objects: *pick* the LID
   Display hidden lines on separate layers<N>: y (Yes)
9. Turn Layers 0, BLADE, BLADE-PH-2, BOTTLE, BOTTLE-PH-2, HANDLE, HANDLE-PH2, LID, and LID-PH2 OFF.
   Note: These layers are those which contain the hidden details of the solid model. In this example there are several layers to turn off

because the model consists of several components – the two pins, the bar and blade as one union; the bottle, lid and handle as separate solid models. The resulting profile drawing is shown in Fig. 8.9.

Work Example 8/6

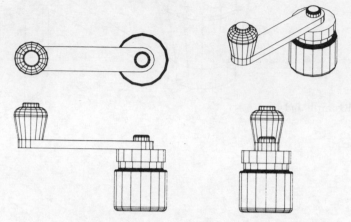

Fig. 8.10 Work Example 8/6

1. **Edit an EXISTING drawing – Main menu**
   Enter NAME of drawing: ex08_04
2. **Layer Control – Settings**
Make a new layer VPORTS – colour green
3. **TILEMODE<1>:**1 0
4. **LIMITS**
Set limits to 0,0 and 420,297
5. **ZOOM** All
6. **MVIEW Fit/2/3/4/Restore//<First Point>:** 4
   Fit/2/3/4: f (Fit)
(Drawing reappears in each of 4 viewports)
7. **MSPACE** (UCS icons reappear in each viewport)
8. Make top left Vport active – move arrow into the viewport and press the *pick* button of the selection device
9. **VPOINT** 0,0,1
10. Make bottom left viewport active
    VPOINT 0,−1,0
11. Make top right viewport active
    VPOINT −1,−1,1
12. Make bottom right viewport active
    VPOINT −1,0,0
13. In each viewport in turn
    ZOOM 1

Note: A zoom scale of 0.8 may be necessary.

14. **PSPACE** (UCS icons disappear; paperspace icon reappears)

15. **MOVE**

Move each viewport to a suitable position (Fig. 8.10)

This involves placing the pick box over one of the lines surrounding the viewport to be moved in response to the Select objects: prompt of the MOVE command. The whole viewport, with its drawing, can then be moved under the control of the selection device.

16. **Layer Control – Settings**

Make Layer 0 the current layer

17. **LINE**

Add a suitable border and title block

18. **TEXT**

Add title in ROMANS style with text 8 units high

19. **MVIEW**

 ON/OFF/Hideplot/Fit/2/3/4/Restore/: h (Hideplot)

 ON/OFF: on

 Select objects: *pick* the **edges** of each viewport in turn

20. **Layer Control – Settings**

Turn Layer VPORTS off

21. **SAVE** ex08_06

22. **PLOT** (plot to plotter) or **PRPLOT** (print to printer)

Work Example 8/7

1. **1. Begin a NEW drawing** – Main Menu

 Enter name of drawing: ex08_07

2. (xload"ame")

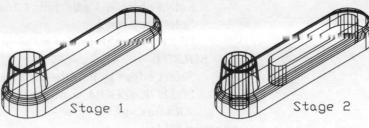

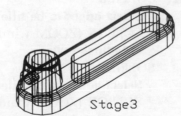

Fig. 8.11 Stages in constructing Work Example 8/7

Stage 1 (Fig. 8.11)
1. **SOLBOX**
   Corners 100,100 and 300,150; **Height** 20
2. **SOLCHP**
   Select solid: *pick* SOLBOX
   Color/Delete/Evaluate/Instance/Move/Next/Pick/Replace/
   Size/eXit/<N>: c (Colour)
   New color?<7 White>: red
   Color/Delete/Evaluate/Instance/Move/Next/Pick/Replace/
   Size/eXit/<N>: x (eXit)
   Command:
3. **SOLBOX**
   Corners 105,105,20 and 295,145,20; **Height** 3
4. **SOLCHP**
   Select solid: *pick* last drawn SOLBOX
Change colour to Yellow
5. **SOLCONE**
   <Center point>: 125,125,23
   <Radius>: 20
   Height of cone: 200
6. **SOLCHP**
   Select solid: *pick* last drawn SOLBOX
Change colour to Green
7. **SOLBOX**
   Corners 105,105,50 and 145,145,50; **Height** 200
8. **VPOINT** −1,−1,1
9. **ZOOM** in a zoom window as large as possible
10. **SOLSUB**
    Select objects: *pick* SOLCONE
    Select objects: 1 selected, 1 found
    Select objects: *Ret*
    Objects to subtract from them: *pick* last SOLBOX
11. **SOLFILL**
    Select edges to be filleted: *pick* vertical corners of large
    SOLBOX (ZOOM window if necessary)
    <Radius>: 25
12. **SOLFILL**
    Select edges to be filleted: *pick* vertical corners of thinner
    SOLBOX (ZOOM window if necessary)
    <Radius>: 20
13. **SOLFILL**
    Select edges to be filleted: *pick* top straight edges of larger
    SOLBOX (ZOOM window if necessary)

<**Radius**>: 5

14. **SOLFILL**
    Select edges to be filleted: *pick* rounded edges of larger
    SOLBOX (ZOOM window if necessary)
    <**Radius**>: 5

15. **SOLFILL**
    Select edges to be filleted: *pick* top edge of SOLCONE
    (ZOOM window if necessary)
    <**Radius**>: 2

16. **SOLUNION**
    Select objects: *pick* all solids drawn

17. **SAVE** ex08_07

Stage 2 (Fig. 8.11)

1. **SOLCYLINDER**
   <**Center point**>: 125,125
   <**Radius**>: 10
   Height of cylinder: 50

2. **SOLCHP**
   Select solid: *pick* last drawn SOLCYLINDER
Change colour to Green

3. **SOLSUB**
Subtract cylinder just drawn from the main solid

4. **SOLCYLINDER**
   <**Center point**>: 275,125; <**Radius**>: 10; **Height:** 23

5. **SOLCYLINDER**
   <**Center point**>: 180,125; <**Radius**>: 10; **Height:** 23

6. **SOLBOX**
   Corners 180,115 and 275,135; **Height** 23

7. **SOLUNION**
   Select objects: *pick* the two SOLCYLINDERS and SOLBOX
   just drawn

8. **SOLCHP**
   Select solid: *pick* SOLUNION just formed
Change colour to Green

9. **SOLSUB**
   Select objects: pick main SOLUNION
   Select objects: 1 selected, 1 found
   Select objects to be subtracted: *pick* smaller SOLUNION

10. **SAVE** ex08_07

Stage 3 (Fig. 8.11)

1. **SOLBOX**
   Corners 105,115,15 and 115,135,15; **Height** 30

2. **SOLCHP**

Select solid: *pick* last drawn SOLBOX

Change colour to Green

3. **ZOOM** window of last drawn SOLBOX
4. **SOLFILL**
    Select edges: *pick* upper edges of last drawn SOLBOX
    <Radius> of fillet: 10
5. **SOLUNION**

Join last drawn box to main solid

6. **VPOINT** from **DISPLAY**

Select **Plan**

7. **UCSFOLLOW<0>:** 1
8. **ZOOM** 1
9. **UCS** 3 (3 point)
    Origin point <0,0,0>: 125,200
    Point on positive portion of X-axis: 125,30
    Point on positive-Y portion of the UCS X-Y plane:
    125,200,100
10. **ZOOM** window as large as possible
11. **SOLCYLINDER**
    <Center point>: 75,35 (centre of fillets of last drawn
    SOLBOX)
    <Radius>: 5
    Height of cylinder: 20
12. **SOLCHP**
    Select solid: *pick* last drawn SOLCYLINDER

Change colour to Green

13. **SOLSUB**

Subtract the last drawn SOLCYLINDER from the main solid.

14. **VPOINT** −1,−1,1
15. **SOLMESH**

Solmesh the whole solid

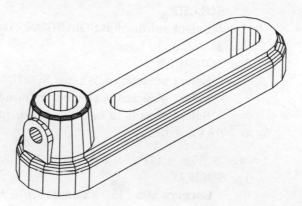

Fig. 8.12 Work Example 8/7

16. **SAVE** ex08_07
17. **HIDE**
18. **SHADE** – This is to try out this command

Work Example 8/8

1. **2. Edit an EXISTING drawing** – Main Menu
   Enter name of drawing: ex08_07
2. (xload"ame")
3. **TILEMODE<1>:** 0
4. **Layer Control – Settings**
Make a new layer VPORTS, colour yellow
5. **MVIEW** f (Fit)
6. Turn Layer VPORTS off. Make layer 0 current
7. **MSPACE**
8. **SOLPROF**
   Select objects: pick the solid model
   Display hidden profile of separate layer <N>: y (Yes)
9. **Layer Control – Settings**
Turn Layer 0 and 0-PH-2 off
10. **SAVE** ex08_08

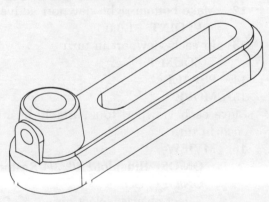

Fig. 8.13 Work Example 8/8

Work Example 8/9

1. **1. Edit an Existing drawing** – Main Menu
   Enter name of drawing: ex08_07
2. (xload"ame") – if necessary
3. **TILEMODE<1>:** 0 Screen changes to paperspace
4. Set limits to 0,0 and 420,297 and Zoom All
5. Make a new layer VPORTS, colour yellow
6. **MVIEW**
   Fit/2/3/4/Restore//<First Point>: 4

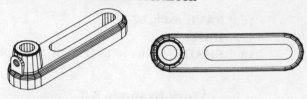

Fig. 8.14 Work Example 8/9

Fit/2/3/4: f (Fit)
(Drawing reappears in each of 4 viewports)
7. **MSPACE** (UCS icons reappear in each viewport)
8. Make top left Vport active – move arrow to the viewport and press the *pick* button of the selection device
9. **VPOINT** 0,0,1
10. Make bottom left viewport active
    VPOINT 0,−1,0
11. Make top right viewport active
    VPOINT −1,−1,1
12. Make bottom right viewport active
    VPOINT −1,0,0
13. In each viewport in turn
    ZOOM 1
14. **PSPACE**
15. **MOVE**
Move each viewport to a suitable position, by *picking an edge of each in turn*
16. **MVIEW**
    ON/OFF/Hideplot/Fit/2/3/4/Restore: h (Hideplot)
    ON/OFF: ON
    Select objects: select an edge of each viewport in turn
17. Turn layer VPORTS off and make layer 0 current
18. Add borders and title
19. **SAVE** ex08_09

Work Example 8/10

1. **2. Edit an Existing drawing** – Main Menu
   Enter NAME of drawing: ex08_07
2. (xload"ame") – if necessary
3. **TILEMODE<1>:** 0

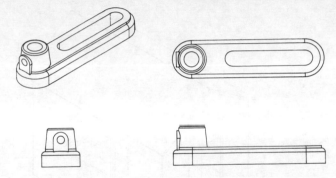

Fig. 8.15 Work Example 8/10

4. Set limits to 0,0 and 420,297 and Zoom All
5. **MVIEW**
     Fit/2/3/4/Restore//<First Point>: 4
     Fit/2/3/4: f (Fit)
(Drawing reappears in each of 4 viewports)
5. **MSPACE** (UCS icons reappear in each viewport)
6. Make top left Vport active — move arrow to the viewport and press the *pick* button of the selection device
7. **VPOINT** −1,−1,1
8. Make bottom left viewport active
     VPOINT −1,0,0
9. Make top right viewport active
     VPOINT 0,0,1
10. Make bottom right viewport active
     VPOINT 0,−1,0
11. In each viewport in turn
     ZOOM 1
12. **PSPACE**
13. **MOVE**
Move each viewport in turn to a suitable position
14. **MSPACE**
15. **SOLPROF** each viewport in turn
16. Turn layers 0; 0-PH-2; 0_PH-3; 0_PH-4; 0-PH-5 and VPORTS off
17. **SAVE** ex08_10
18. **PLOT** or **PRPLOT**
   Note: Both the SOLPROF and the plotting or printing of all four viewports will take a considerable time to complete.

Work Example 8/11

This Work Example demonstrates how Layers and UCS planes can

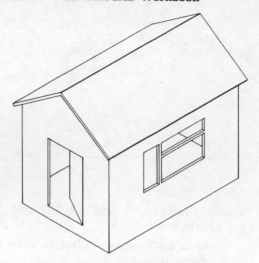

Fig. 8.16 Work Example 8/11

be changed in order to ensure that constructions are in the correct plane and that different colours assist in determining where parts of the overall drawing are on screen.

1.   **1. Begin a NEW drawing** – Main Menu
        Enter NAME of drawing: ex08_10
2.   (xload"ame")
3.   **LIMITS**
Set limits to 594,420 (A3 sheet size)
4.   **ZOOM** All
5.   **UCSFOLLOW<0>:** 1
6.   **UCS CONTROL – Settings**
        pick **Define new current UCS** – new dialogue box appears
        Name SIDES
        pick **Origin, Xaxis, Plane** – dialogue box disappears
        Origin point: 150,0
        Point on positive portion of the X-axis: 450,0
        Point on positive-Y portion of the UCS X-Y plane: 150,0,100
7.   **UCS Origin/ZAxis/3point/Entity/View/X/Y/Z/Prev/Restore/**
        Save/Del/<World>: w (World)
8.   **UCS CONTROL – Settings**
        pick **Define new current UCS** – new dialogue box appears
        Name FRONT
        pick **Origin, Xaxis, Plane** – dialogue box disappears
        Origin point: 150,0
        Point on positive portion of the X-axis: 150,300
        Point on positive-Y portion of the UCS X-Y plane: 150,0,300
9.   **ZOOM** All

10. **Layer Control – Settings**
    Make Layers:
    SIDES – colour Magenta
    FRONT – colour Yellow
    ROOF – colour Red

Note: We now have three UCS planes – *WORLD*, SIDES and FRONT. These can be set either from UCS Control in the Settings pull-down menu or by typing r (Restore) in answer to the UCS command prompts followed by the UCS plane name. We also have three layers, each of which can be made current by selection from Layers Control in the Settings pull-down menu. Layer 0 will also be available.

11. Make Layer 0 current
12. Make *WORLD* the current UCS and ZOOM 1

Note: In the following, coordinates can be either picked on screen with the aid of .XY filter followed by typing the Z coordinate when (need Z): appears, or typed in full at the keyboard. Some heights will have to be typed.

13. **SOLBOX**
    Corners 150,0,20 and 450,200,20; **Height** 5
14. Make SIDES the current layer
15. **SOLBOX Corners** 150,0 and 155,200; **Height** 200
16. Make SIDES the current UCS and ZOOM 1
17. **COPY**
    Select objects: *pick* last drawn SOLBOX
    <Base point of displacement>: 0,0
    Second point of displacement: 295,0
18. Make FRONT the current UCS and **ZOOM** 1
19. Make FRONT the current layer
20. **SOLBOX**
    Corners 0,0 and 5,200; **Height** 300
21. **PLINE From point:** 0,200
    To point: 100,270
    To point: 200,200
    To point: c (close)
22. **SOLEXT**
    Pick pline or circle: *pick* last drawn PLINE
    Height of extrusion: 5
    Extrusion taper angle from Z <0>: *Ret*
23. **COPY**
    Select objects: *pick* last drawn SOLBOX
    <Base point of displacement>: 5,0
    Second point of displacement: 200,0

24. **UCS Control**

Make SIDES the current UCS and **ZOOM** 1

25. **COPY**

Copy the EXTRUSION from 0,200 to 295,200

26. **VPOINT** −1,−1,1

To check constructions so far

27. **UNDO** to undo the VPOINT

28. **SAVE** ex08_10 (a precautionary save)

29. **UCS Control**

Make FRONT the current UCS and ZOOM 1

30. **UCS Control – Settings**

Make a new UCS LEFTROOF at points: 0,200; 100,270; 0,200,100

31. Make ROOF the current layer

32. **SOLBOX**

> **Corners** −10,310 and 125,−10; **Height** −5

33. Make FRONT the current UCS

34. **UCS Control – Settings**

Make a new UCS RIGHTROOF at points: 200,200; 100,270; 200,200,100

35. **SOLBOX**

> **Corners** −10,310 and 130,−10; **Height** 5

36. Make FRONT the current UCS

37. **SOLBOX**

> **Corners** 60,25 and 140,160; **Height** 5

38. Make *WORLD* the current UCS

39. **SOLMOVE**

> **Select objects:** *pick* last drawn SOLBOX
>
> **<Motion description>:** e (edge)
>
> **Select edge to define coordinate system:** *pick* lower edge of SOLBOX
>
> **<Motion description>/?:** rx-30

40. Make FRONT the current UCS

41. **SOLBOX**

> **Corners** 60,25,−1 and 140,160,−1; **Height** 7

42. **SOLSUB**

Subtract doorway SOLBOX from front SOLBOX

43. Make SIDES the current UCS

44. **SOLBOX**

> **Corners** 80,160,1 and 220,80,1; **Height** −7

45. **SOLSUB**

Subtract last drawn box from the side

46. Make SIDES the current UCS

47. **ZOOM**

48. **SOLBOX**
    Construct SOLBOXes as in Fig. 8.16 – each bar being 5 wide and −5 high
49. **SOLUNION**
    SOLUNION the two window bars
50. **VPOINT** −1,−1,1
51. **SOLUNION**
    pick each part of the construction in turn to SOLUNION the whole solid model
52. **SOLMESH**
53. **HIDE**
54. **SAVE** ex08_11

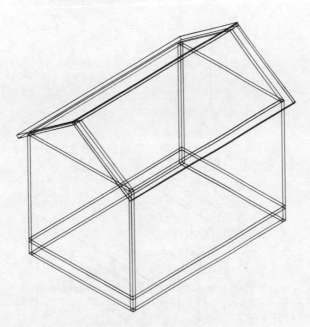

Fig. 8.17 First stage of Work Example 8/11

Work Example 8/12

Amend the drawing for Work Example 8/10 to add a porch, porch windows and doorstep as shown in Fig. 8.19.

Work Example 8/13

1. **1. Begin a NEW drawing** – Main Menu
   Enter name of drawing: ex08_12
2. (xload"ame")
3. **UCSFOLLOW<0>:** 1
4. **CIRCLE**

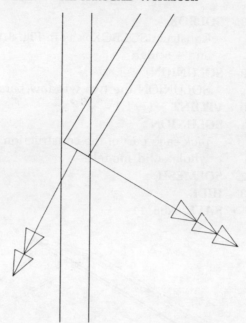

Fig. 8.18 The SOLMOVE
icon in position after e
(edge)

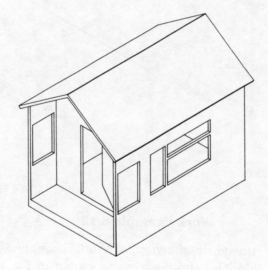

Fig. 8.19 Work Example 8/12

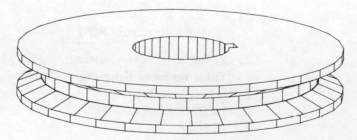

Fig. 8.20 Work Example 8/13

        <Center point>: 200,160
        <Radius>: 100

5. **SOLVAR**
        Variable name or ?: solwdens
        Wireframe mesh density (1 to 8> <4>: 8

Note: This sets the solid variable so that the mesh density is greater than the normally used density.

6. **SOLEXT**
        Select objects: *pick* the CIRCLE
        Height of extrusion: 5
        Extrusion taper angle <0>: *Ret*

7. **ELEV**
        New current elevation <0>: 5
        New current thickness <0>: *Ret*

8. **CIRCLE**
        <Center point>: 200,160,5
        <Radius>: 100

9. **SOLEXT**
        Select objects: *pick* the CIRCLE
        Height of extrusion: 6
        Extrusion taper angle <0>: 60

10. **ELEV**
        New current elevation <0>: 11
        New current thickness <0>: 4

11. **CIRCLE**
        Same centre as 4 above with Radius 85

12. **ELEV**
        New current elevation <0>: 0
        New current thickness <0>: 0

13. **UCS Control – Settings**
        Make a new UCS CENTRAL at points: 200,250; 200,50; 200,250,100

14. **ZOOM** 1

15. **MIRROR**
        Select objects: w (window) – window the whole model *Ret*
        First corner: Other corner: 3 found
        First point of mirror line: Mirror line taken along
        Second point of mirror line: top line of model
        Delete old objects <N>: *Ret*

16. **ZOOM** use a window to fill the screen with the model

17. **SOLUNION**
        SOLUNION all six objects

18. Make *WORLD* the current UCS

19. **SOLCYLINDER**
    <Center of cylinder>: 200,160
    <Radius>: 30
    Height of cylinder: 40
20. **SOLBOX**
    Corners 195,195 and 205,185; **Height** 40
21. **SOLUNION**
    SOLUNION the last drawn SOLBOX and SOLCYLINDER
22. **SOLSUB**
    SOLSUB the last SOLUNION from the whole model
23. **SOLMESH**
24. **VPOINT** 4,−1,1
25. **HIDE**
26. **SAVE** ex08_13

Work Example 8/14

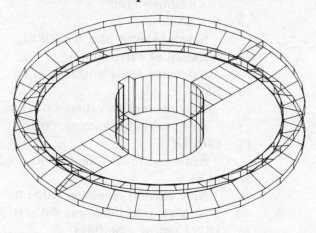

Fig. 8.21 Work Example 8/14

This Work Example shows how a sectional cut can be made across an AME solid model. The SOLVARIABLES controlling the hatching are − SOLHPAT controls the pattern of hatching; SOLHSIZE the spacing of the hatch pattern; SOLHANGLE the angle of the hatching.

1. 2. **Edit** and **EXISTING drawing** − Main Menu
   Enter name of drawing: ex08_13
2. (xload"ame")
3. **UCSFOLLOW<0>**: 1
4. **UCS *WORLD***
5. **UCS CONTROL − Settings**
   pick **Define new current UCS** − new dialogue box appears

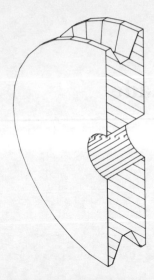

Fig. 8.22 Another sectional view through the pulley

Name SECTION
pick **Origin, Xaxis, Plane** – dialogue box disappears
Origin point: 100,160
Point on positive portion of the X-axis: 300,160
Point on positive-Y portion of the UCS X-Y plane: 100,160,100

6. **SOLHANGLE <0>:** 90
7. **SOLHPAT <NONE>:** ansi31
8. **SOLHSIZE <1>:** 2
9. **SOLSECT**
   Select objects: *pick* the solid model
10. **VPOINT** −1,−1,1
11. **SAVE** ex08_14

Note: Figure 8.22 shows a similar pulley wheel which has been sectioned, but which is a solid of revolution through an included angle of 180°. Compare this with the results of Work Example 8/14.

CHAPTER 9

Dview and AutoShade

Dview

Introduction

The DVIEW command allows dynamic pictorial viewing of our 3D and solid models. The command can be called:

1. by typing dview or its abbreviation dv;
2. selecting DVIEW from the DISPLAY on-screen menu;
3. selecting Dview from the Display pull-down menu;
4. selecting DVIEW from the VIEW menu area of the graphics tablet overlay.

The Work Examples employing DVIEW in this chapter allow the reader to experiment with the various prompts of the command. These are listed at the command line after the objects to be viewed have been selected:

CAmera/TArget/Distance/POints/PAn/Zoom/TWist/CLip/Hide/Off/Undo/<eXit>:

Note: Dview will only operate in MSPACE or when TILEMODE is on (1).

Work Example 9/1

1. **Main Menu   1. Begin a NEW drawing**
   Enter NAME of drawing: ex09_01
2. Construct the drawing of the table as shown in Fig. 9/1 within screen limits of 210,148 (A5 sheet size)
3. **SAVE** ex09_01

Work Example 9/2

1. **Main Menu   2. Edit an Existing drawing**

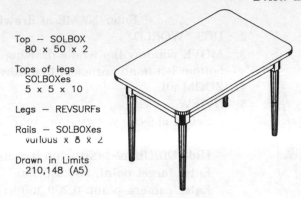

Top — SOLBOX
80 x 50 x 2

Tops of legs
SOLBOXes
5 x 5 x 10

Legs — REVSURFs

Rails — SOLBOXes
various x 8 x 2

Drawn in Limits
210,148 (A5)

Fig. 9.1 Work Example 9/1

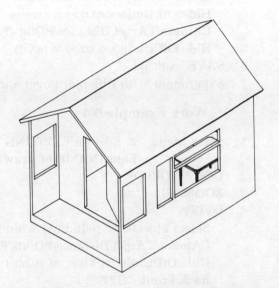

Fig. 9.2 Work Example 9/2

Enter NAME of drawing: a:\ex08_12

Note: This is the drawing of a hut, with added porch, windows and doorstep from Work Example 8/12 from the previous chapter.

2. Add shelves as in Fig. 9.4. These are SOLBOXes of width 9 and height 2 and of any suitable length, at heights of 100, 135 and 170

3. **SOLUNION** pick the original hut drawing and the SOLBOXes making up the shelves

4. **INSERT** insert the table (Work Example 9/1) in any convenient position inside the hut

5. **SAVE** ex09_02

Work Example 9/3

1. **Main Menu   2. Edit an EXISTING drawing**

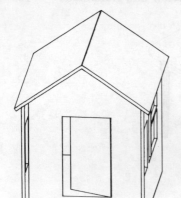

Fig. 9.3 Work Example 9/3

Enter NAME of drawing: ex09_02

2. **UCS** *WORLD*
3. **MOVE** window the whole drawing and move so that the bottom left-hand corner of the drawing is at 350,150
4. **ZOOM** all
5. **DVIEW**

    Select objects: w (window) window the whole drawing
    CAmera/TArget/Distance/POints/PAn/Zoom/TWist/CLip/Hide/Off/Undo/<eXit>: po (points)
    Enter target point: 500,250,150
    Enter camera point: 0,200,300
    CAmera/TArget/Distance/POints/PAn/Zoom/TWist/CLip/Hide/Off/Undo/<eXit>: h (Hide)
    CAmera/TArget/Distance/POints/PAn/Zoom/TWist/CLip/Hide/Off/Undo/<eXit>: x (eXit)

6. **SAVE** ex09_03
7. Experiment with different target and camera points

Work Example 9/4

1. **Main Menu   2. Edit an EXISTING drawing**
    Enter NAME of drawing: ex09_03
2. **UCS** *WORLD*
3. **ZOOM** all
4. **DVIEW**

    Select objects: w (window) window the whole drawing
    CAmera/TArget/Distance/POints/PAn/Zoom/TWist/CLip/Hide/Off/Undo/<eXit>: cl (CLip)
    Back/Front/<OFF>: f
    Eye/ON/OFF/<Distance>: −10 (or move slider appearing at the top of the screen with the selection device until the figure −10 shows at the status line) x (eXit)
    CAmera/TArget/Distance/POints/PAn/Zoom/TWist/CLip/Hide/Off/Undo/<eXit>: x (eXit)

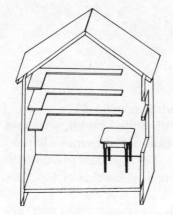

Fig. 9.4 Work Example 9/4

5. **HIDE**
6. **SAVE** ex09_04
7. Experiment with different clip points, either keying figures for distances or by picking with the selection device from the slider which appears at the top of the screen. Experiment with both Front and Back clip points

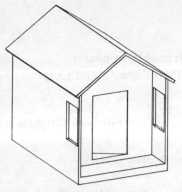

Fig. 9.5 Work Example 9/5

Work Example 9/5

1. **Main Menu   2. Edit an EXISTING drawing**
   Enter NAME of drawing: ex09_02
2. **UCS** *WORLD*
3. **ZOOM** all
4. **DVIEW**
   Select objects: *Return* (and the **dviewblk** appears)

Note: The **dviewblk** regenerates much more quickly when dragged around the screen than a drawing such as ours will. This allows quicker and easier selection of viewing positions when employing the Camera, POints, TArget or other **DVIEW** command options.

**CAmera/TArget/Distance/POints/PAn/Zoom/TWist/CLip/
Hide/Off/Undo/<eXit>:** TA (target)

Experiment by moving the slider which appears for adjusting vertical position (slider on right of screen) and horizontal position (slider at top of screen). Press *Return* when satisfied.

**CAmera/TArget/Distance/POints/PAn/Zoom/TWist/CLip/
Hide/Off/Undo/<eXit>:** x (eXit)

Note: The door and window of our Work Example do not coincide with the positions of the door and windows of the **dviewblk** drawing.

5. **HIDE**
6. **SAVE** ex09_05

Work Example 9/6

1. **Main Menu   2. Edit an EXISTING drawing**
   Enter NAME of drawing: ex09_02

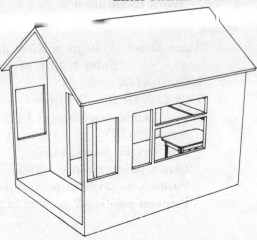

Fig. 9.6 Work Example 9/6

2. **UCS** *WORLD*
3. **ZOOM** all
4. **DVIEW**
    Select objects: *Return* (and the **dviewblk** appears)
    CAmera/TArget/Distance/POints/PAn/Zoom/TWist/CLip/
    Hide/Off/Undo/<eXit>: pa (PAn)
    Pan the **dviewblk** into a central position on screen
5. **CAmera/TArget/Distance/POints/PAn/Zoom/TWist/CLip/Hide/**
    Off/Undo/<eXit>: po (POints)
    Enter target point: *Return* (accept figures given)
    Enter camera point: 60,250,200
    CAmera/TArget/Distance/POints/PAn/Zoom/TWist/CLip/
    Hide/Off/Undo/<eXit>: d (Distance)
    New target/camera distance: adjust slider to approx 3X
Note: Perspective icon appears bottom left of screen

    CAmera/TArget/Distance/POints/PAn/Zoom/TWist/CLip/
    Hide/Off/Undo/<eXit>: ca (CAmera)

Adjust sliders to give a reasonable perspective drawing on screen
6. **CAmera/TArget/Distance/POints/PAn/Zoom/TWist/CLip/Hide/**
    Off/Undo/<eXit>: x (eXit)
7. **HIDE**
8. **SAVE** ex09_06

AutoShade

Work Example 9/7 is included here to demonstrate how the stand
alone software programme AutoShade can be used to give a shaded,
coloured view of 3D models.

Work Example 9/7

Stage 1
1. **Main Menu   1. Begin a NEW drawing**
              Enter NAME of drawing: a:\vase
2. **UCSFOLLOW<<0>**: 1
3. **UCS CONTROL – Settings**
    pick **Define new current UCS**
    Name FRONT
    pick **Origin, Xaxis, Plane**
    Origin point<0,0,0>: 0,150
    Position on positive portion of X-axis: 420,150
    Point on positive-Y portion of the UCS X-Y plane: 0,150,100

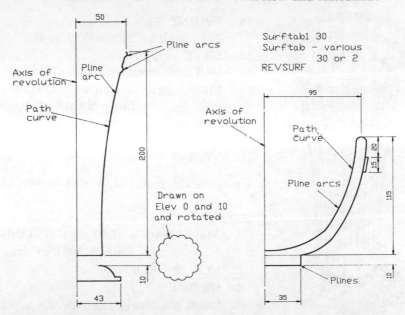

Fig. 9.7 Stage 1 of Work
Example 9/7

4. **ZOOM** 1
5. **PLINE**
   Draw the outlines of the vase (Fig. 9.7) in plines. The two
   small arcs should be separate from the main arc
6. **LINE**
   Draw the axis of revolution line
7. **UCS** *WORLD*
8. **ELEV**
   Set elevation to 0 and 10
9. **PLINE**
   Draw the wavy edge base
10. **UCS**
    Restore the FRONT UCS and, if necessary move the wavy
    edge pline to its correct position in relation to the plines
    drawn in the FRONT UCS
11. **Surftab1** – set to 30
12. **Surftab2** – set to 30
    Note: These settings for Surftab are for the main arc. Re-set
    Surftab2 to 2 when applying REVSURF to the two smaller arcs and
    the base.
13. **REVSURF**
    Pick each of the pline arcs in turn to form solids of revolution
14. **ERASE**
    Erase the axis of revolution

15. **VPOINT** −1,−1,1
    The resulting pictorial view is shown in Fig. 9.8
16. **SAVE** a:\vase
17. **QUIT** followed by y (Yes)
18. **Main Menu   2. Edit an EXISTING drawing**
                Enter NAME of drawing: a:\bowl
19. In a similar manner form a solid of revolution from the bowl outline given in Fig. 9.7 and save it as a:\bowl
20. **VPOINT** −1,−1,1

The resulting pictorial view is shown in Fig. 9.9.

Stage 2

1. **Main Menu   2. Edit an EXISTING drawing**
               Enter NAME of drawing: a:\vase
2. **UCS** *WORLD*
3. **INSERT**
   Insert the bowl drawing
4. **EXPLODE**
   Explode the bowl drawing
5. **SCALE**
   Window the vase and scale it to 0.5. Window the bowl and scale it to 0.3
6. **MOVE**
   Move the bowl drawing to a suitable position in relation to the vase drawing
7. **MOVE**
   Move the vase and bowl to a position near to the top right-hand corner of the screen as shown in Fig. 9.10
8. **3DFACE**
   Draw a rectangle around the vase and bowl as in Fig. 9.10
   Note: Now check whether the two 3D models and the rectangle

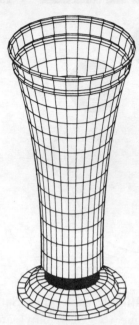

Fig. 9.8 Vpoint view of the vase for Work Example 9/7

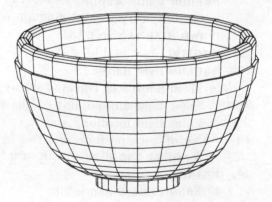

Fig. 9.9 Vpoint view of the bowl for Work Example 9/7

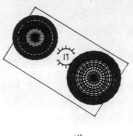

Fig. 9.10 Work Example 9/7

are in their correct vertical positions in relation to each other. Set a FRONT UCS plane and, if necessary, move the vase, bowl and rectangle. Then revert to UCS *WORLD*.

9. **ASHADE**
   Wait until ashade.lsp loads

10. **LIGHT**
    Enter light name: L1
    Point Source or Directed <P>: *Return*
    Enter light location: .xy
    .xy of: *pick* position as in Fig. 9.10
    (need Z): 150

11. **LIGHT**
    Enter light name: L2
    Point Source or Directed <P>: D *Return*
    Enter light aim point: *pick* between vase and bowl
    Enter light location: .xy
    .xy of: *pick* position of L2 as in Fig. 9.10
    (need Z): 150

12. **LIGHT**
    Enter light name: L3
    Point Source or Directed <P>: D *Return*
    Enter light aim point: *pick* between vase and bowl
    Enter light location: .xy
    .xy of: *pick* position of L3 as in Fig. 9.10
    (need Z): 130

13. **CAMERA**
    Enter camera name: C1

> **Enter target point:** *pick* between vase and bowl
> **Enter camera location:** .xy
> **.xy of:** *pick* position of C1 as in Fig. 9.10
> **(need Z):** 130

14. **ACTION**
    SCENE
    Enter scene name: S1
    Select the camera: *pick*
    Select a light: *pick* L1
    Select a light: *pick* L2
    Select a light: *pick* L3 *Return*
    Select scene location: *pick* and scene details appear (Fig. 9.10)

15. **FILMROLL**
    File – a:\ex09_07

Note: In order to view the contents of the file a:\ex09_07.flm, it is necessary to load the stand-alone software for AutoShade and open the file while in AutoShade. The results of this are shown in Plate 16 (in colour section). Figure 9.11 is a pictorial view in line drawing form of the vase and bowl on their rectangle.

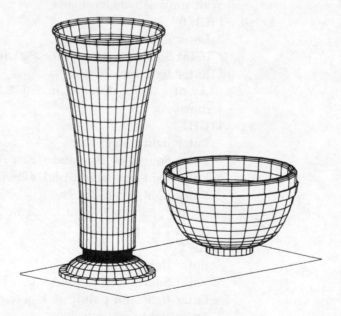

Fig. 9.11 Vpoint view of scene for Work Example 9/7

Further examples of AME solid model drawing

Two further examples of AME solid model drawings are shown in Figs 9.12, 9.13 and 9.14. These are not given here as Work

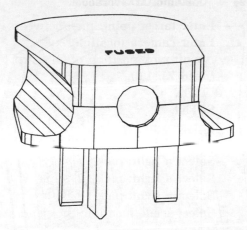

Fig. 9.12 Solid model
drawing of a three-pin plug

Examples, but as examples of solid models which involve a number
of AME primitives and AME commands. Figure 9.12 is a 3D model
of a 13 Amp electric plug. Figure 9.13 shows a number of different
views of the solid as seen from different DVIEW directions. Figure
9.14 is a solid model drawing of a wall telephone. This last
illustration includes the pline outline from which the body of the
telephone solid model drawing was extruded.

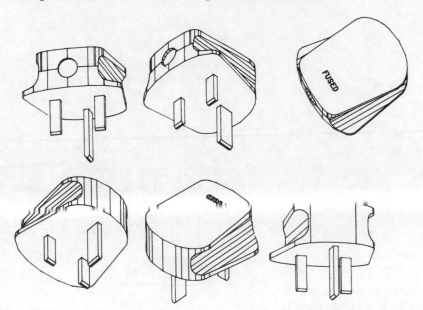

Fig. 9.13 Pictorial views of
the three-pin plug as seen
from different TArget points
of DVIEW. Bottom right
drawing is a SOLPROF view

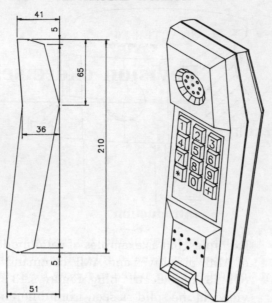

Fig. 9.14 Solid model of a
telephone handset

CHAPTER 10

Revision exercises

Introduction

This chapter contains ten exercises for revision purposes. No assistance is given in any of the exercises. Readers attempting these exercises are required to follow their own sequences of operations.

Exercise 10/1

Figure 10.1 shows a Golden Mean Spiral. The spiral consists of a series of quadrants based on Golden Mean rectangles, each rectangle having sides in the proportion 1:1.618. Construct the spiral to any suitable sizes.

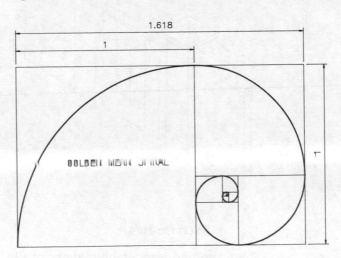

Fig. 10.1 Exercise 10/1

Exercise 10/2

Draw the badge Fig. 10.2.

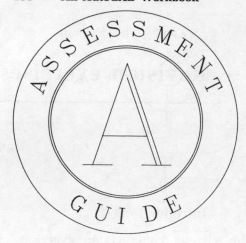

Fig. 10.2 Exercise 10/2

Exercise 10/3

Figure 10.3 shows an isometric drawing of a gate within supports, together with parts of a fence. Working to any convenient dimensions copy the drawing.

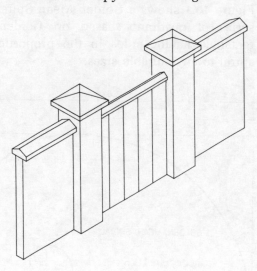

Fig. 10.3 Exercise 10/3

Exercise 10/4

Copy the two orthographic views of Fig. 10.4 and add a sectional end view. Work to a scale of full size within a screen set to limits of 420,300.

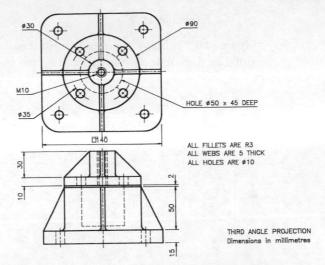

ø30   ø90

M10

HOLE ø50 x 45 DEEP

ø35

ⵁ140

ALL FILLETS ARE R3
ALL WEBS ARE 5 THICK
ALL HOLES ARE ø10

30

10

2

50

15

THIRD ANGLE PROJECTION
Dimensions in millimetres

Fig. 10.4 Exercise 10/4

Exercise 10/5

Figure 10.5 shows 3D solid model drawings of two wine glasses. Draw the two models to suitable sizes.

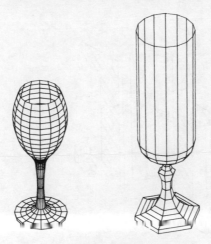

Fig. 10.5 Exercise 10/5

Exercise 10/6

Copy the drawing Fig. 10.6, working to suitable dimensions.

Fig. 10.6 Exercise 10/6

Exercise 10/7

Figure 10.7 shows two 3D solid model drawings. Working to suitable dimensions construct the two model drawings.

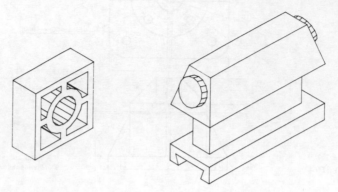

Fig. 10.7 Exercise 10/7

Exercise 10/8

Figure 10.8 is a 3D solid model construct in AME. Construct the model drawing to any suitable dimensions.

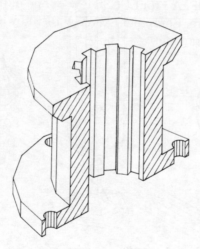

Fig. 10.8 Exercise 10/8

Exercise 10/9

Figure 10.9 is a 3D solid model drawing of a bearing bracket constructed in AME and then acted upon by the AME command SOLPROF. Copy the bracket to any suitable dimensions.

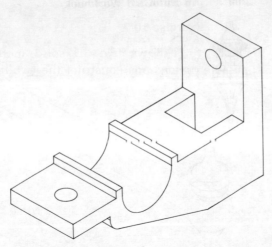

Fig. 10.9 Exercise 10/9

Exercise 10/10

Figure 10.10 is a 3D solid model of a decorative hanger drawn in AME. Construct the hanger to suitable dimensions. Figure 10.11 shows the bracket of Exercise 10/10 after using the AME command SOLPROF. A Front UCS view of one of the end units is included in this figure. Complete Exercise 10/10 by applying SOLPROF to your model drawing.

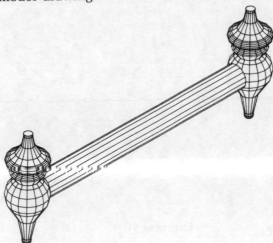

Fig. 10.10 Exercise 10/10

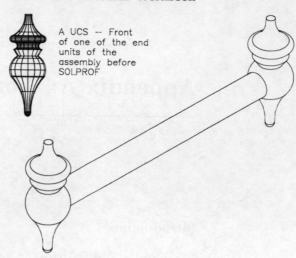

A UCS — Front
of one of the end
units of the
assembly before
SOLPROF

Fig. 10.11 Exercise 10/10
after SOLPROF

Appendix A: Work drawing file

Introduction

When the AutoCAD **Main Menu** appears and

1. Begin a NEW drawing

a prompt **Enter NAME of drawing:** appears

the required filename is entered and the Main Menu is replaced by the AutoCAD drawing editor. The drawing screen is usually then configured to certain parameters by the automatic loading of a file acad.dwg from the standard AutoCAD software. If this file is configured so that the limits of the drawing editor are (0,0) and (420,297) – suitable for drawing for A3 sheet size drawings – then the majority of Work Examples in this book can be constructed without any amendments being made to the drawing editor. When working in an AutoCAD drawing editor configured in this way, it is advisable to turn Grid points, Coords and Snap on by pressing the F7, F8 and F9 keys.

If, however, a different file to acad.dwg is loaded when beginning a NEW drawing, it is advisable to make up your own drawing file in which to construct the Work Examples.

It is possible by selecting the Main Menu item

5. Configure AutoCAD

to configure so that your own drawing file is the one which appears in the drawing editor when beginning a NEW drawing. This would be acceptable if you were the only operator using the computer, but if others also use the computer, doing so could cause other operators some difficulty.

A drawing file work.dwg

This file sets the AutoCAD drawing editor so that Work Examples constructed within it and plotted full size (scale 1:1) will produce A3 sheet size plots, in which each coordinate unit will be equal to 1 mm. When it is loaded work.dwg sets the following parameters for the AutoCAD drawing editor:

1. Screen coordinate limits set to x,y top right = 420,297;
2. Layers on which drawings can be constructed:
        0 – for outlines;
        Hidden – for hidden detail;
        Centre – for centre lines;
        Text – for text and dimensions;
3. Linetypes for each of the layers:
        Continuous – layers 0 and Text;
        Hidden – hidden detail;
        Center – centre lines;
4. Colours for each of the layer linetypes:
        White – outlines (layer 0);
        Red – hidden detail (layer hidden);
        Green – centre lines (layer center);
        Cyan – text (layer text);
5. Metric dimensioning variables;
6. Grid set to 10 and on; Snap set to 5 and on; Coords on;
7. Border lines and a title block.

The method of constructing this drawing file is described below. Figure A1 shows the resulting drawing. Do NOT include the figures of Fig. A1 in the drawing.

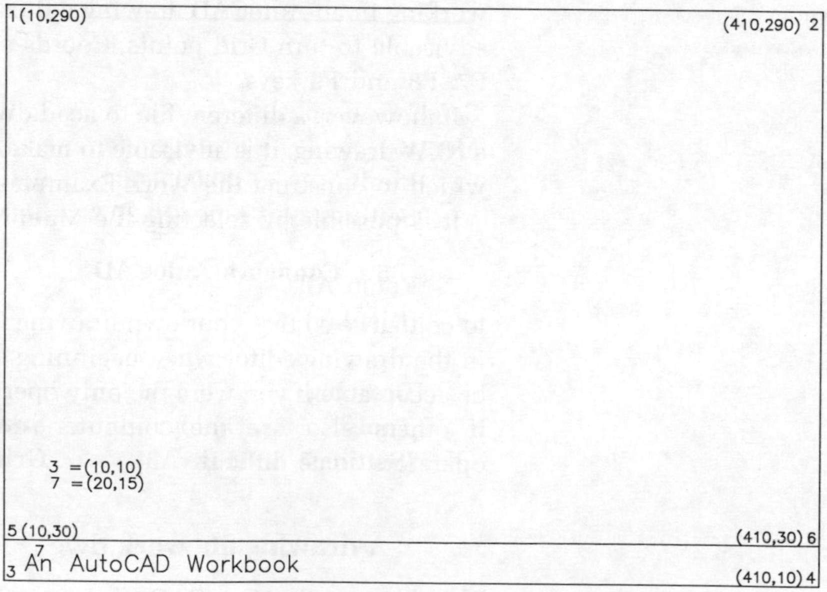

Fig. A1 The Work drawing for preparing Work Examples

Warning

When constructing a Work Example, it is advisable to save to disk at regular intervals to avoid losing constructions when, e.g., power fails, software programme crashes. When using work.dwg on which to construct drawings, be careful to save to a filename other than work. Failure to observe this precaution will result in your constructions being saved to the filename work.dwg. Next time work.dwg is loaded as an existing drawing, the previous fully constructed drawing will appear on screen.

Stages in forming a work.dwg file

1. From **Main menu** select **1. Begin a New drawing**
2. At the prompt **Enter name of drawing:** a:\work *Keyboard Return*

Note: Do not include the extension *.dwg.*

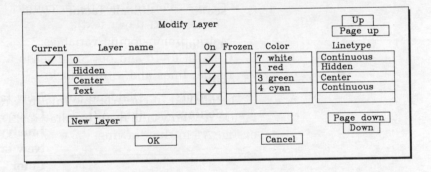

Fig. A2 The Modify Layer dialogue box

Select Pull-down Menu	Prompts/Action		Result
1. **Limits Settings**	**<0,00,0,00>**	Return	
	Key 420,297	Return	Limits 420,297
2. **Zoom All (Display)**			Screen redraws to limits
3. **Drawing Tools (Settings)**	Dialogue box (Fig. A3)	**Snap** – 5 **Grid** – 10	Snap set to 5

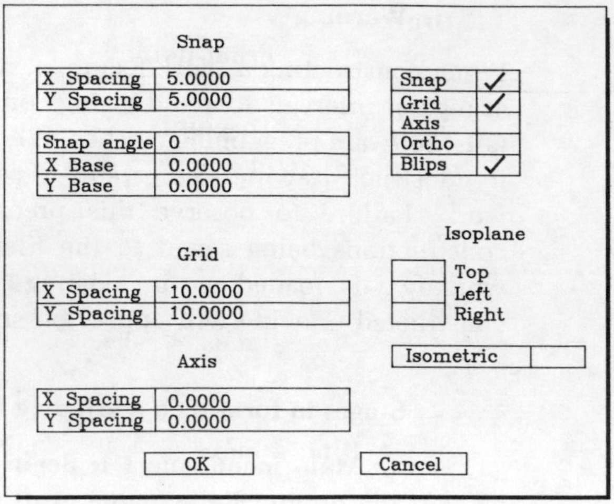

Fig. A3 The Drawing Tools
dialogue box

		pick **OK**	Grid set to 10
4.	**Linetype scale** (**Options**)	**Scale factor** 0.5	Linetypes scales set for A3 sheet sizes
5.	**Layer Control** (**Settings**)	Dialogue box (Fig. A2)	**New layer** – centre **Color** – green **Linetype** – center **New layer** – hidden **Color** – red **Linetype** – hidden **New layer** – text **Color** – cyan *pick* **OK**
			3 new layers set
6.	**Draw** **Line**	From point: *pick* 1 **To point:** *pick* 2 **To point:** *pick* 4 **To point:** *pick* 3 (10, 10) **To point:** c (close)	

7. **Draw**
   Line   From point:
                      pick 5
                      To point:
                      pick 6   Borders
                                                                drawn

Type at Keyboard	Command line	Type at Keyboard	Result
8. dim	**Dim:**	dimasz	
	Dim: dimasz	4	Dimension arrows set to 4 units
		dimexe	
	Dim: dimexe	4	Extension above dimension line set to 4 units
		dimexo	
	Dim: dimexo	4	Extension line starts 4 units from drawing outline
		dimtih	
	Dim: dimtih	off	Text horizontal
		dimtad	
	Dim: dimtad	on	Text above dimension line
		dimtoh	
	Dim: dimtoh	off	Text outside dimensions in line with dimension text
		dimtol	
	Dim: dimtol	off	No tolerances included
Exit			Command line reverts to **Command:**

9. Press function key F6 – Switches Coords On/Off. Command line states <**Coords off**> or <**Coords on**>. Make sure Coords in on.

10. style   **Style**
            Text style name (or ?): romans *Keyboard Return*
            Font file: romans *Keyboard Return*
            Height: 8 *Keyboard Return*
            Width factor <**1.0000**>: *Return*
            Obliquing angle <**0**>: *Return*
            Backwards? <**N**>: *Return*
            Upside-down? <**N**>: *Return*
            Vertical? <**N**>: *Return*
            ROMANS is now the current text style.
            Command:

11. dtext   **Start point** *pick* 7(20,15)
             Rotation angle <0>: *Return*
             Text:
     An AutoCAD Workbook Text appears on screen

12. save   **File name**
             <A:\WORK>:   *Return*   Screen clears and file
                                          work.dwg is saved to disk
                                          in drive a:

Notes

AutoCAD can be configured so that a file (usually acad.dwg) is automatically loaded when item 1 is selected from the **Main Menu** and the required filename, as in the following example, typed in response to the prompt:

Enter NAME of drawing: a:\ex02_01

when the drawing ex02_01 is saved, it will be automatically saved as ex02_01.dwg, despite the fact that the loaded drawing file was acad.dwg.

This does NOT apply when your work.dwg is loaded as an EXISTING drawing. If working on your own work.dwg, the filename, e.g. ex02_01, must be given at the prompt:

Command: save *Keyboard Return*
Filename <A:\WORK>: ex02_01 *Keyboard Return*

and your drawing will be saved as ex02_01.dwg on the disk in drive a:\.

Note that the filename must be typed into the Create drawing file dialogue box which appears when save is typed at the command line.

It is possible that the file acad.dwg will, when automatically loaded, provide a suitable A3 size AutoCAD drawing editor, in which to construct the Work Examples (as described above – page 201). If this is so, there is no need to load a work.dwg file. It is however unlikely that the sheet borders and title block carrying the title An AutoCAD Workbook will be found in an acad.dwg file. However it is an easy matter to add the borders, title block and title, if the acad.dwg file does load a suitable A3 size sheet into the AutoCAD drawing editor.

Appendix B: Menu trees

The two illustrations in this Appendix have been reproduced here with permission from Autodesk (UK) Limited.

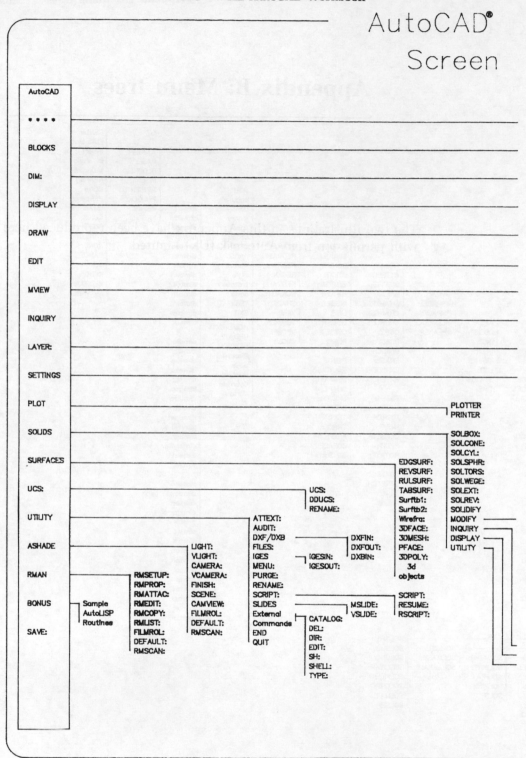

Fig. B1 On-screen menu tree

Release 11 Menus

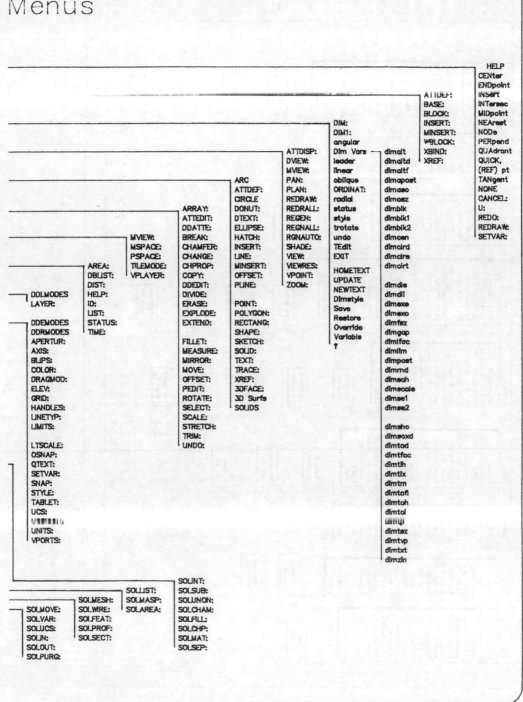

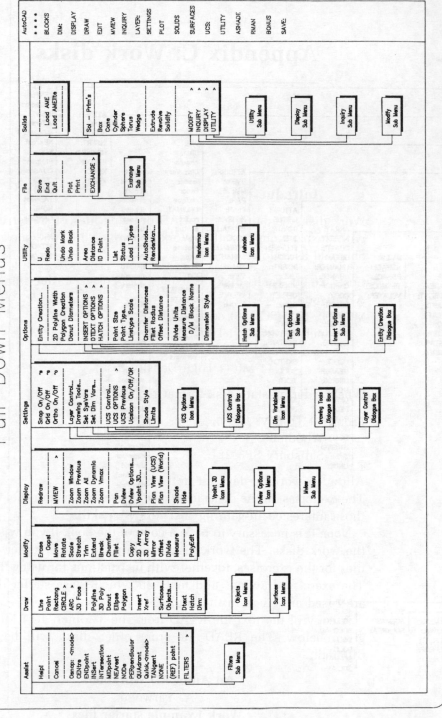

Fig. B2 Pull-down menu tree

Appendix C: Work disks

Introduction

Work disks containing AutoCAD drawing files of starter drawings with instructions for the Work Examples in this book can be obtained as follows:

Cost: £6.00 **each** disk. Cheques or Postal Orders payable to A.Yarwood.
MS.DOS IBM PC(386) compatible
    5¼ inch – 1.2 Kb (1 High Density disk);
    3½ inch – 720 Kb (2 Double Density disks), or
               – 1.44 Mb (1 High Density disk).

When ordering state disk format required.

From: 10 Tinneys Close,
       Woodfalls,
       Salisbury SP5 2LU.

Allow 15 working days for delivery.
The exercises on the disks form a comprehensive course of work for those interested in gaining CAD drawing skills

Note: It is necessary to have a copy of the book if you wish to use the work disks. The work disks contain AutoCAD starter drawing files for the exercises, together with instructions for using the disks. The exercise drawings and texts on which these starter drawings are based are given in the book.

A copy of the text file READ from the 3½ inch 1.44 Mb disk is given below. The READ file from other disks will be slightly different:

An AutoCAD Workbook
A. Yarwood
Work Example starter files

Before working with this disk, copy its contents to another formatted disk using either e.g.:

> DISKCOPY A: A if copying to the same drive in which the disk is held or e.g.:
> XCOPY A: B:/S if copying between two disk drives.

The files from this disk can only be loaded into the drawing editor of AutoCAD Release 11 or a later release.
WARNING: Do **NOT** save your work on this disk.
Note: It is advisable to copy the directory containing the file being worked from this floppy disk to the hard disk of your computer and load the file into the AutoCAD drawing editor from the hard disk in order to work the Example.

If this is not possible, load the file being worked from this floppy disk, but do NOT save to this floppy disk. Save to the hard disk. Failure to observe this rule may result in the loss of the drawing file being worked.

This disk holds a number of AutoCAD drawing files. The files are held in directories with names such as CHAP02, corresponding with a chapter number in the book.

The drawing files have names such as EX01.DWG, corresponding to a Work Example number in a chapter.

When a drawing file from this disk is loaded into the AutoCAD drawing editor some instructions appear on screen. Follow these instructions. The instructions will be on a layer named TEXT. By turning Layer TEXT off and turning other layer(s) – usually Layer 0 – on, the instructions will disappear from the screen and a 'starter' drawing will appear in their place. To complete the Work Example from the 'starter', follow the description of processes given in the relevant pages of the book.

To construct a Work Example from one of the drawing files:

1. start up the computer;
2. load AutoCAD – usually by typing ACAD;
3. when the AutoCAD Main Menu appears select:
    > **2. Edit an EXISTING drawing**
4. when the prompt:
    > **Enter NAME of drawing:** appears
5. type the name of the drawing file required, an example being:
    > **Enter NAME of drawing:** chap02\ex01

    This includes the directory (chap02) and the filename (ex01). The backslash (\) must be included. Do NOT include the filename extension (.dwg). If loading from this disk, an example could be:

Enter NAME of drawing: a:\chap02\ex01

This includes the name of the floppy disk drive;

6. Follow the instructions which appear in the drawing editor when the drawing file has been loaded.

WARNING: When the Work Example currently being constructed has been completed, save the result to the hard disk of the computer **NOT** to this floppy disk. Then type QUIT followed by Y (yoo) to got back to tho AutoCAD Main Monu. Do **NOT** typo END when your work is finished because this will attempt saving the work to the disk from which the drawing file was originally loaded.

Contents of this disk

There are 62 AutoCAD drawing files in 7 directories and a text file held on this disk. These are:

CHAP02 – 6 drawing files EX01.dwg to EX06.dwg;
CHAP03 – 6 drawing files EX01.dwg to EX06.dwg;
CHAP04 – 9 drawing files EX01.dwg to EX09.dwg;
CHAP05 – 10 drawing files EX01.dwg to EX10.dwg;
CHAP06 – 9 drawing files EX01.dwg to EX09.dwg;
CHAP07 – 9 drawing files EX01.dwg to EX09.dwg;
CHAP08 – 13 drawing files EX01.dwg to EX13.dwg;
READ – These notes

Note: The drawing files in CHAP07 and CHAP08 can only be worked if the software for the Advanced Modeling Extension (AME) has been loaded.

The text file READ can be read on screen by typing the following at the keyboard.

If the disk in the disk drive A: – at the prompt A:

A:\> type read

The text file READ can be printed on a printer by typing the following at the keyboard.

A:\> type read > prn

Index